Tony Monahan

An Empathetic Approach to Physical Education Teacher Education

Tony Monahan

An Empathetic Approach to Physical Education Teacher Education

LAP LAMBERT Academic Publishing

Impressum / Imprint

Bibliografische Information der Deutschen Nationalbibliothek: Die Deutsche Nationalbibliothek verzeichnet diese Publikation in der Deutschen Nationalbibliografie; detaillierte bibliografische Daten sind im Internet über http://dnb.d-nb.de abrufbar. Alle in diesem Buch genannten Marken und Produktnamen unterliegen warenzeichen-, marken- oder patentrechtlichem Schutz bzw. sind Warenzeichen oder eingetragene Warenzeichen der jeweiligen Inhaber. Die Wiedergabe von Marken, Produktnamen, Gebrauchsnamen, Handelsnamen, Warenbezeichnungen u.s.w. in diesem Werk berechtigt auch ohne besondere Kennzeichnung nicht zu der Annahme, dass solche Namen im Sinne der Warenzeichen- und Markenschutzgesetzgebung als frei zu betrachten wären und daher von jedermann benutzt werden dürften.

Bibliographic information published by the Deutsche Nationalbibliothek: The Deutsche Nationalbibliothek lists this publication in the Deutsche Nationalbibliografie; detailed bibliographic data are available in the Internet at http://dnb.d-nb.de. Any brand names and product names mentioned in this book are subject to trademark, brand or patent protection and are trademarks or registered trademarks of their respective holders. The use of brand names, product names, common names, trade names, product descriptions etc. even without a particular marking in this works is in no way to be construed to mean that such names may be regarded as unrestricted in respect of trademark and brand protection legislation and could thus be used by anyone.

Coverbild / Cover image: www.ingimage.com

Verlag / Publisher:
LAP LAMBERT Academic Publishing
ist ein Imprint der / is a trademark of
AV Akademikerverlag GmbH & Co. KG
Heinrich-Böcking-Str. 6-8, 66121 Saarbrücken, Deutschland / Germany
Email: info@lap-publishing.com

Herstellung: siehe letzte Seite /
Printed at: see last page
ISBN: 978-3-8443-9553-2

Zugl. / Approved by: Kingston, University of Rhode Island, Diss 2010

TABLE OF CONTENTS

1

APPENDICIES

LIST OF TABLES

CHAPTER 1: INTRODUCTION, STATEMENT OF THE PROBLEM,

JUSTIFICATION FOR SIGNIFICANCE OF THE STUDY

The purpose of this research study was to determine if college students studying in Physical Education Teacher Education (PETE) could increase empathy levels as a result of a semester-long educational intervention. Four groups of students were studied from three East-coast, U.S. universities, two groups of subjects constituted the experimental groups and two constituted the control groups. After agreeing to participate in the study by signing an IRB-approved informed consent document (Appendix A), all subjects were given the Davis Interpersonal Reactivity Index (IRI) (Davis, 1980), a scale designed to measure the cognitive and affective components of empathy (Appendix B), at the beginning and end of the spring 2009 semester. In addition, all students were given an essay assignment at the beginning of the spring, 2009 semester (Appendix C). Students were given the same essay assignment at the end of the spring 2009 semester plus a reflection assignment (Appendix D). A complete transcript of subject essays and reflections is provided in Appendix E.

In addition to regular course content, participants in the experimental groups participated in a curricular intervention involving an emphasis on empathy and affective educational practices. Participants in the control groups participated in regular course content. At the end of the spring, 2009 semester, data was collected and analyzed to see if changes occurred between pre and post measures, and between experimental and control groups. Results are discussed in Chapter 4.

Statement of the problem

This study focused on the problem of declining health among youth in the United States and the overall inability of traditional physical education (PE) programs to adequately address this situation. It has been suggested that generations of students have been "turned off" to lifelong physical activity because of their experiences in school-based PE, which were frequently characterized by failure and humiliation (Carlson, 1995; Grineski & Bynum1996; Portman, 1995; Robinson, 1990; Walling & Martinek, 1995). If students are to use what they have learned in PE in order to maintain lifelong fitness, negative experiences associated with PE needs to change. Incorporating an empathetic instructional approach in PE may facilitate more positive experiences for students and bring about a greater chance to impact the long-term health of participants. To bring about this change, modifications in PE teacher education are indicated.

It has been argued that many PE teacher education candidates choose PE because of a passion for sports (Fox, 1988; Gard, 2006). This passion is often fueled by competitive success and supported by coaches, teammates, and other like-minded classmates and friends. As a result, PE is often viewed as "a profession that talks and teaches to itself" (Gard, 2006. p. 2). Dewar & Lawson (1984) further examined this trend in their study of subjective warrant - the perception of what is required to enter a given profession (Lortie, 1975), which

plays a large part in candidates' choice of teaching. Teaching candidates tend

to place interpersonal qualities at the forefront of their subjective warrant. In

regards to PE, teaching candidates tend to be attracted to the profession

because of extensive involvement and success in PE and athletic experiences

during K-12 schooling, consideration of themselves as top PE students, and

perception of themselves as high achievers in sports (Dewar & Lawson, 1984).

Traditional PE (historically referred to as "gym class") has generally focused

on sports and competition, repetition of skills, calisthenics, and a social

hierarchy favoring athleticism. Unfortunately, this approach benefits some

students over others, as described by Smith & Cestaro (1998).

> "For many students, this [traditional] teaching technique has meant
> three weeks of frustration. The education of the high achievers (the
> good athletes) suffers because of the inability of their lesser-talented
> classmates to function at as high a level. The lesser-talented students in
> a particular unit cannot improve their skills because of limited
> opportunities for contact with balls or other objects – thus limiting their
> opportunities for success – during traditional games. Students who
> dislike a particular unit often just tune out, not helping themselves, their
> classmates, or their teachers" (Smith & Cestaro, 1998, p. 3).

The crisis in childhood obesity and other inactivity-related disorders speaks

to the need for PE teachers to reach all students, not just those who exhibit the

same passion or relate to competitive conquest. If the ultimate goal of PE is the

realization of a physically fit society (AAHPERD, 1999; NASPE, 2004), then

the PE challenge would be *success for all*. This appears to be contrary to the

traditional PE model.

Many researchers and educators have called for a change in thinking in PE away from the traditional model to a more humanistic, or student-centered one (Blitzer, 1995; Corbin, 2002; Grineski, 1992; Locke, 1992; Smith & Cestaro, 1998; Tishman & Perkins, 1995; Williams, 1994). Borrowing from the work of Rogers (1983), PE teachers who embody a humanistic approach should be genuine (have congruence), have positive regard for their students, and exhibit empathic understanding of them in order to establish a supportive and advantageous learning environment.

If many PE pre-service teachers are indeed the athletically elite and competitively-triumphant, a concentrated effort will be needed to convert them into teachers of *all* children. Such a progression of thinking requires reference to cultural examples and situations, problem-solving exercises, experiences and reflection (Donaldson 1978). Positive change can also be influenced by committed and caring teachers, empathetic and reflective to the needs of athletically diverse students (Cothran, 2001; Page & Scanlan, 1994; Robinson, 1990; Rovengo & Bandhauer, 1997).

Justification for significance of the study

This section will discuss three specific reasons to support further investigation of the problem. First presented are studies demonstrating the reliability and applicability of the measurement instrument selected for this study, the IRI (Davis, 1980). Second, a review of other research studies involving efforts to improve empathy through an educational intervention will

6

be presented. Third, a case will be presented for empathy research in the area of physical education teacher education, which has not been attempted before.

1. The Interpersonal Reactivity Index (IRI) has been shown to be a reliable instrument in measuring empathy as a multidimensional construct of empathy in several fields of study.

    The IRI has been utilized as a measurement instrument in a wide range of research fields including psychology (Davis, 1983; Davis & Franzoi, 1991), counseling (Hatcher et al., 1994), medicine (Bellini et al., 2002), corrections (Bush, et al., 2000), and education (Espelage et al., 2003). It has been cited as "by far the most widely used instrument" to assess empathy (Pulos et al., 2004, p. 355). In a study that assessed and compared empathy and perspective-taking instruments (Iannotti, 1985), the IRI was given the highest ratings for reliability and validity, rating 3 out of 3 which meant "consistently easy to administer; high statistical reliability; strong validity scores." Davis (1980) reported good internal reliabilities with standardized alpha coefficients ranging from .71 to .79 for the four subscale measures and test-retest reliability ranging from .61 to .81 over an eight to ten week period.

    Davis (1983) conducted a study involving college students in an effort to establish "convergent and discriminable validity" (p. 114) of the IRI subscales: Empathic concern scale (EC), Fantasy scale (FS), Perspective Taking scale (PT), and the Personal Distress scale (PD). Davis compared IRI results to those of other empathy measures to

7

determine the relationship of each subscale with a psychological construct. Davis hypothesized that there should be "clear differences among the scales in terms of their relationships with other psychological constructs" (p. 114). For example, a high score on the PT scale should be associated with higher social functioning and higher self-esteem, while a high PD score should be inversely related to PT and correlate with lower social functioning and lower self-esteem. The author found that participant PT and EC scores were significantly and positively related (mean $r = .33$) while PT and PD scores were significantly negatively related (mean $r = -.25$).

Davis and Franzoi (1991) investigated changes in empathic tendencies in adolescents over an extended period of time. High school-aged subjects (n = 205) were administered the IRI at one-year intervals for three years. Results indicated year-to-year scores increased in PT, EC, and FS, while PD scores predictably decreased, exhibiting substantial test-retest correlations (.50 to .62) over the three year period. These results were consistent with previous findings and supported Hoffman's (1987) theory of empathy as being a developmental construct.

Furthermore, IRI subscales have been used, either individually or in conjunction with other scales, to measure and predict empathic dispositions in subjects. Oswald (2003) explored Davis's (1980) suggestion that higher level empathy, as represented by the IRI empathic concern (EC) and perspective-taking (PT) subscales, are related to helping behaviors. She investigated whether perspective-taking, as measured by the IRI, was related to helping behaviors in 162 ethnically diverse working adults. She found that participants who took an opportunity to volunteer time counseling others had significantly higher PT scores than those who did not ($t = 2.75, p = .007$).

2. Previous studies have demonstrated that empathy can be augmented by an educational program.

    Kalliopuska and Roukonen (1993) assessed the effects of a three-month holistic empathy education program with musical exercises on the development of empathy in six and seven year-old children (n = 32). The authors found a significant increase in empathy scores between pre and post measurements on the Feshbeck and Roe Empathy Test ($t = -3.5, p < .001$) and concluded that the development of empathy can be accelerated by an educational program.

    Cutcliffe and Cassedy (1999) conducted a short (12 weeks), skills-based college-level counseling course designed for nursing students in an effort to measure the development of empathy among participants. The authors found a significant increase in empathy scores among participants (n = 38) between pre and post measurements on the Ivey et al. empathy rating scale (pre-test $M = 58.34, SD = 11.36$, post-test $M = 71.1, SD = 8.48, p = .001$). The study demonstrated evidence that participant empathy scores can increase during a short skills-based

9

course. However, the authors express the need for more comprehensive study in this area, particularly with use of control groups.

Hatcher et al. (1994) investigated whether the development of empathy could be stimulated by a semester-long educational intervention. The authors noted that previous efforts to "teach" empathy have ignored the concept of empathy as a developmental construct. With a stated interest in empathy as it relates to maturity, the authors used the IRI to investigate pre and post-test differences between high school and college groups (n = 104), and between experimental and control groups (college level only). Experimental groups took classes in peer facilitation skills which included behavioral-attending skills, non-judgmental and empathic listening skills, facilitative feedback, and role-playing exercises. Subjects in the control group took a behavioral psychology course with no peer-facilitation skills. ANCOVAs revealed that the college experimental group improved significantly more than the control group ($t = -2.23, p < .05$). IRI results also indicated that although empathy scores in both high school and college experimental groups improved, the college group improved significantly more in the "most advanced" forms of empathy (perspective taking & empathic concern) than the high school group $F (1, 65) = 5.01, p<.03$. The findings suggest that an educational training component is crucial in developing individuals' ability to listen and communicate empathetically, but this training showed to be more effective in college students than in high school students.

3. What is being proposed has not been done in PE.

This study is designed to examine the empathy construct in physical education teacher education students and determine if a one semester, empathy-based methods course changes empathy levels among them. These questions have not been addressed in physical education teacher education before. Although studies have been conducted on empathy and teacher/counselor education in social work (Pinderhughes, 1979), counseling (Hatcher et al., 1994; Kremer & Dietzen, 1991), cultural studies (Cruz & Patterson, 2005; Goodman, 2000; McAllister & Irvine, 2002), and music education (Kalliopuska & Roukonen, 1993), no previous studies have been found in the field of PE. In recent years, strides have been made to improve both curriculum and assessment in PE in order to improve students' physical activity levels (AAHPERD, 1999; NASPE, 2004). Concurrent with these developments, there is a need for pre-service PE teachers to develop and practice affective traits aimed at fostering a productive relationship with students. "[I]t is time to realize that the preparation of teachers for the schools of the next century consists of educating human teachers in human relationships" (Patterson & Purkey, 1993, p. 147).

In the broadest sense, education, as practiced in a democracy, must make provisions so that all students have an opportunity to succeed (Dewey, 1944).

11

With regards to PE, the challenge is to ensure that all students have an opportunity to lead a healthy, physical life. An increase of empathic development in teacher education may allow PE pre-service teachers to understand better the needs of their students, and thus better design programs that accommodate them.

Research on teaching practice demonstrates multiple factors contribute to teaching excellence. In addition to specific teaching skills and subject-matter knowledge, affective characteristics such as enthusiasm, perseverance, and concern for children are essential for good teaching and lifelong learning (Darling-Hammond & Sykes, 2003). However, affective attributes are largely ignored (Gerdes, 2001; Laker, 1996; Noblit et al., 1995; Noddings, 1992, 1998; Patterson & Purkey, 1993) or, at best, tacitly implied (Anderson, 2002; Brown et al., 2000) in today's educational reform efforts. Without specific attention devoted to development of affective qualities, teachers may not have sufficient experience or training to properly recognize student needs, or display understanding and empathy for their students' unique situations.

Study's importance to the advancement of knowledge and its significance to the student

This study attempts to answer the United States Department of Health and Human Services (USDHHS) (2000) call to address and overcome barriers inhibiting the acquisition and maintenance of healthy lifestyles, as well as the USDHHS *Healthy People 2010* goals of 1) to help individuals increase quality and years of healthy life, and 2) to eliminate health disparities among different

12

segments of the population (USDHHS, 2000) by setting the stage for increased physical activity among students in PE classes. Research exhibits the myriad of ways physical fitness is beneficial to students. The effort to humanize PE is directed toward making students feel more comfortable, confident, and supported in their PE experience. A good physical education program is one that not only engages students in physical activity but prepares them to engage in physically healthy activities throughout life (Siedentop & Locke, 1997). PE is essentially a socially-based class where students have an opportunity to practice the dynamics of cooperation and competition, group work, communication, problem solving, leadership skills, and character development (Gerdes, 2001; Laker, 1996, 2000; NASPE, 2001; Solomon, 1997; Whitehead, 2000). Participating students could possibly benefit from an empathetic teacher who exhibits a sense of possibility for all.

Stating that the desire to be cared for is a universal human characteristic, Noddings (1995) asserted that a major objective for responsible schools is not only the practice of caring for students but the development of a caring capacity in them. The development of the human capacity is considered to be essentially linked with the development of cognitive intelligence (Stout, 1999). In addition, the capability of empathy is considered essential to the development of social responsibility (Berman, 1998). It is conceivable that focused empathy lessons and activities could lead PE pre-service teachers to develop deeper humanistic qualities, such as caring for and empathic understanding of their students, while also serving to aid in the development of

13

character and moral citizenship. It is also conceivable that the students of our future teachers would benefit from this empathetic awareness as well. Research has shown that empathic response affects both the empathizer *and* the target (Håkansson & Montgomery, 2003). Because empathy entails identifying and understanding the feelings of others in a helping capacity, it is considered a potential neutralizer of powerlessness (Pinderhughes, 1979). While teachers develop better ways to understand and help students through empathetic practice, students also gain by being helped and supported, which could alleviate fears of failure and helplessness, increase motivation, and even help to advance their own empathy development.

In essence, this study was conceived as an awakening of critical consciousness and an attempt at what Freire (1983) referred to as conscientization – a conscious endeavor to transform the world. The ultimate goal in PE is a physically fit society. Therefore, the PE challenge is *success for all*, which will require reciprocal communication, critical thinking, problem-solving strategies, understanding, and empathy in order to accommodate the needs of every student – from the physically elite to the physically challenged.

CHAPTER 2: REVIEW OF LITERATURE

Context

This review covers, from general to specific, the overall circumstances that have led to this study. First presented is research delineating the decline in health for both domestic and international populations. Second, as many health issues are preventable, research is presented on the health benefits of physical activity. However, traditional PE does not benefit all students, which may lead some to avoid physical activity because of negative experiences. Third, research is presented that outlines these issues in the PE class, including 3.a. competition, 3.b. student perceptions, including social status, and 3.c. learned helplessness. Finally, the chapter concludes with research on empathy in education and its potential relevance to the PE class.

Health/fitness decline

One of the vital issues facing society today is the decline of human health and fitness (AOA, 2002; CDC, 1997; USDHHS, 2000; WHO, 2007). The United States is currently experiencing a growing epidemic of preventable diseases such as obesity, where the number of obese adolescents has more than doubled in the past 25 years (AOA, 2002). Worldwide, one billion people are overweight or obese, a figure that is expected to reach 1.5 billion by 2015 (WHO, 2007). There is an international epidemic of chronic diseases, such as coronary heart disease (CHD), obesity, stroke, and cancer. For example, the World Health Organization (WHO) projects the CHD death toll, presently 17

15

million each year, to increase. Although most are preventable chronic diseases are the leading cause of death in the world (USDHHS, 2000; WHO, 2007).

Many factors contribute to the epidemic in preventable, chronic diseases, such as technological advances, tobacco use, the abundance of unhealthy food choices, and other unhealthy habits (USDHHS, 2000; WHO, 2007). However, a leading cause seems to be physical inactivity. In the United States, only 15 percent of adults engage in regular vigorous physical activity, and 40 percent do not engage in regular physical activity at all. Physically inactive people are twice as likely to develop CHD as those with active lifestyles (USDHHS, 2000). The noted decline in children's health coincides with a decrease in PE programs, as well as a decrease in student participation in PE during secondary school (Corbin, 2002; Satcher, 2005; USDHHS, 2000). There are also indications that an increasing number of students find PE boring, irrelevant, and unpleasant, likely contributing to the noted decrease in participation (Carlson, 1995; Grineski & Bynum, 1996; Tinning & Fitzclarence, 1992).

Although serious, the situation of an unhealthy society is conceivably fixable; with appropriate knowledge and resources the trend can be reversed. In order to achieve the goal of a healthy society, innovative methods and theories that endeavor to help all children toward a self-maintained, healthy lifestyle are needed.

Benefits of physical activity

Research indicates that physical activity is central to a healthy mind and body (Jensen, 2005; Satcher, 2005; Sosa, 1995; Symons et al., 1997; USDHHS, 2000). After reviewing 25 key reports from 1989-1991, the National Action Plan for Comprehensive School Health Education (consisting of representatives from the American Cancer Society and over 40 health education and social service organizations) concluded that student health and achievement "are inextricably intertwined" and healthy children are in a better position to learn in school (Symons et al., 1997). These researchers also found evidence suggesting that exercise is associated with improved academic outcomes (class grades, standardized test performance, attendance and graduation rates), improved student behaviors, and positive interpersonal relationships while also reducing the incidence of depression, anxiety and fatigue.

In 2005, the California Department of Education (CDE) reported "a strong positive relationship between physical fitness and academic achievement" (p. 6). Their findings validated earlier California studies (CDE, 2001; Satcher, 2005) and demonstrated a positive significant relationship between student physical fitness scores and achievement in all grades (5, 7, 9) measured. The cumulative evidence of the CDE study indicated that "conditions that improve general health promote both a healthy body and improved intellectual capacity" (CDE, 2005, p. 6). Additionally, a study examining the relationship between physical fitness and academic achievement (grades 3 & 5, $n = 259$)

17

found that physical fitness levels – specifically aerobic capacity – were positively related to academic achievement, as measured by the ISAT standardized achievement test in mathematics and reading (Castelli, et. al, 2007).

Regular physical activity, even at moderate levels, is known to reduce the risk of CHD, hypertension, colon cancer, and diabetes, as well as increase bone strength and lean muscle, decrease body fat, enhance psychological well-being, and reduce symptoms of depression (USDHHS, 1996; USDHHS, 2000). In addition, research suggests that physical activity - even at moderate levels - increases brain function and nervous system development (Sosa, 1995). Studies of the cerebellum indicate that movement is linked to learning through enhanced sensory input, visual-spatial skills, and long-term recall (Jensen, 2005; Sosa, 1995). "In the same way that exercise shapes up the muscles, heart, lungs, and bones, it also strengthens the basal ganglia, cerebellum, and corpus callosum, all key areas of the brain" (Jensen, 2005, p. 85).

PE has the potential to be the most important and effective school subject in promoting students' healthy and active lifestyles (DeCorby et al., 2005; Janzen, 2003/2004; Siedentop & Locke, 1997). Since it is now known that movement and exercise are important to brain development and learning (Jensen, 2005; Sosa, 1995), one of the challenges in PE is to incorporate more movement and exercise into school programs (AAHPERD, 1999; Ciccomascolo & Riebe, 2006; Grineski & Bynum 1996; King, 1991; Locke, 1992; NASPE, 2004; Stelzer, 2005).

18

Traditional PE does not benefit everyone

In 2000, the U.S. Department of Health and Human Services (USDHHS) called on public education to identify and address the barriers that inhibit the acquisition and maintenance of healthy lifestyles in various populations. Despite its potential to develop physically active lifestyles, PE has historically focused on calisthenics, athletic skill proficiency and competitive sports and games (McCallum, 2000; Portman, 2003; Villaire, 2001; Williams, 1992; Virshup, 1999). These traditional programs tend to meet the needs of students who are athletically elite or physically gifted, while alienating others to PE and ultimately to physical activity altogether (Carlson, 1995; Grineski & Bynum, 1996; Stevens-Smith, 2002; Virshup, 1999). Indeed, the traditional model of PE has been unsuccessful in promoting physically active and fit adults (Grineski & Bynum, 1996; Portman, 2003; Villaire, 2001; Westcott, 1992).

A report released by the Centers for Disease Control and Prevention (CDC, 1997) stated that participation in physical activity declines through adolescence. In 1997, nearly half of America's teenagers were not vigorously active on a regular basis, and over one-third were physically inactive for more than four days a week. Corbin (2002) contended that the observed decline of students' participation in PE (see CDC, 1997; USDHHS, 2000) was partly due to the fact that PE teachers often chose a traditional sports curriculum out of convenience rather than a more challenging curriculum that fit the present (and future) needs of their students. Corbin presented a 1999 survey of secondary PE programs showing that the top five PE activities were team sports

19

(basketball, volleyball, baseball/softball, football, soccer). The only PE activities on the list that could be considered lifetime activities were one middle school activity (jogging, listed eighth) and three high school activities (weight training, jogging, calisthenics, listed sixth, seventh, and eighth respectively).

On the other hand, a 1996 USDHHS survey of the most popular adult physical activities revealed no team sports in the top ten and only one competitive sport (tennis, listed tenth) on the list (Corbin, 2002; USDHHS, 1996). This polarity between what is practiced by adults and what is taught to children has led some to consider the prolongation of the traditional PE program to be an educational and health "crisis" (Locke, 1992; Tinning & Fitzclarence, 1992). Others have called the loosely-coupled relationship between PE teacher education programs and cooperating schools that uphold the sports model a systemic failure (Siedentop & Locke 1997). Locke (1992) argued that replacing the dominant program model of PE (required attendance, mandatory dress, lack of student choice, content based on instructor interest) is the only course of action that will save PE.

"Old-style PE excludes kids who aren't natural athletes. It tends to focus on games where the least skilled students are the first to be eliminated, and thus branded losers, and fails to build skills that kids can actually use" (Graham, as cited in Virshup, 1999, p. 138). Traditional PE is based in the cultural transmission ideology of education. In this approach educators are given the responsibility to transmit to students the knowledge (seen as fixed), skills, social, and moral rules of our culture (Kohlberg & Mayer, 1972). This also

parallels Freire's (1983) concept of "Banking Education" where students are

considered objects, or blank slates, and educators deposit official knowledge

into them, irrespective of their needs and interests. In this concept, "knowledge

is a gift bestowed by those who consider themselves knowledgeable upon

those whom they consider to know nothing" (Freire, 1983, p 72). Students are

only expected to be passive receivers of the teacher's information and do not

take an active part in their education. This disempowerment contributes to

student alienation, disinterest, resistance, and even depression (Kohn, 1998).

Historically, the PE version of cultural transmission was central to

traditional PE where teachers and coaches espoused a tough, authoritarian,

"my way or the highway" mentality (McCallum, 2000; Virshup, 1999;

Williams, 1996). Additionally, instruction and assessment focused on skill

proficiency and competitive success (King, 1991; Virshup, 1999; Westcott,

1992). Such classes did not offer physically and socially inferior students the

same opportunities for having positive experiences as students considered

active and competent (Anderssen, 1993; Carlson, 1995; Dunn et al., 2007;

Grineski & Bynum; 1996, Virshup, 1999). Thus, the cultural transmission

model ostensibly benefits the strong through the domination of the weak. In

addition, this model could be seen as a deterrent to critical thinking, as learning

is limited to the acquisition of "official knowledge," and authority is not to be

questioned (Blitzer, 1995; Freire, 1983; Kohlberg & Mayer, 1972; McBride,

1995; Tishman & Perkins, 1995; Williams, 1996).

21

Central to traditional PE curriculum are the sports-minded "gym teachers" who historically have been viewed as having little or no empathy for students who are not athletically proficient (Bekiari et al., 2005; Duncan et al., 2002; Himberg, 2005; Stork & Sanders, 1996; Williams, 1996). In "gym" class, non-athletic students have been known to suffer the humiliation of being picked last, losing, and playing the role of human targets. In this environment, lesser skilled students may appear indifferent, lazy, or unmotivated because of feelings of failure in competitive situations (Covington, 1985; Dunn et al., 2007; Evans & Roberts, 1987; Fitzpatrick & Watkinson, 2003). This appearance may be a self-protective behavior exhibited because of such feelings (Covington, 1985; Fitzpatrick & Watkinson; 2003; Garner, 1990).

Like many other subjects, PE usually includes a minority of "elite" students, in this case, the athletically elite, who are naturally gifted, highly trained or highly skilled in the subject. The American Council on Exercise (2008) has estimated that as little as ten percent of students are natural athletes who can thrive on athletic competition. The remainder of the class, the majority, will be comprised of students of lesser ability. The impact of elite status in PE may have far-reaching implications; e.g., athletically elite students are often viewed by their peers as more popular than lesser skilled students (Dunn et al., 2007; Evans & Roberts, 1987; Weiss & Duncan, 1992). In addition, those students who enjoy positive PE experiences appear more likely to continue physical activity through adulthood (Portman, 2003; Ferguson et al., 1989). Traditional PE programs, however, tend to meet the perceived needs

22

of these athletically gifted, often at the expense of those not as athletic
(Stevens-Smith, 2002; Stork & Sanders, 1996; Virshup, 1999).

Competition suppresses empathy

Studies on empathy and competition have shown that highly competitive
children were found to have lower empathy scores then less competitive
children (Barnet & Bryan, 1974; Barnett, Matthews, Corbin 1979; Barnett,
Matthews, Howard, 1979; Kohn, 1986). Competition has also been shown to
decrease altruism in elementary school children (Barnett and Bryan, 1974;
Kohn, 1986).

A powerful illustration of this was seen at the October, 2005 annual
meeting of the Rhode Island Association for Health, Physical Education,
Recreation and Dance (RIAHPERD) when conference, keynote speaker and
former NASPE Teacher of the Year, Beth Kirkpatrick spoke about her first PE
teaching position. Although anecdotal, it illustrates many of the points which
underline this study. Mrs. Kirkpatrick began by saying she was a former
college basketball player, and during her first interview for a teaching position,
she assured the principal and superintendent that if she was hired she would
lead the girls' basketball team to the state finals. She made good on her
assurance, as her team won the state championship that year. "I didn't care
about PE," she declared, "All I cared about were my girls. My job was to win
basketball games. In PE, I did nothing. I rolled the balls out and let them play."
Mrs. Kirkpatrick went on to tell us that a few years later, she was conducting

the one-mile run with her students. Standing at the finish line with a stopwatch, she was screaming at her lesser-skilled students to get moving, pushing them to finish. One overweight student, huffing and puffing, reached the finish line and collapsed at Mrs. Kirkpatrick's feet. Her uniform was soaked with sweat and she had blood-blisters on her legs where her shorts were rubbing. There was immediate shock and concern over this girl's health. Mrs. Kirkpatrick told us that she prayed right then and there for the girl to be O.K. (which she was). She went home that night and re-assessed her priorities. She thought of the girl who had never complained, who had always tried her hardest, and she felt embarrassed to have put her through that ordeal. Her epiphany sparked a change in her, which led her to change her classes, her teaching, and her focus. Since, she has been a nationally recognized advocate for children's health.

Mrs. Kirkpatrick's initial lack of concern for her non-athletic students was based in the perception that they weren't "my girls" – the players on her basketball team. Her own competitive success may have contributed to her admitted lack of empathy for all the other students in her classes. In sports, she was a successful basketball player and state-champion coach. However, as a PE teacher, she admittedly paid little attention to the non-athletic students in her classes. She probably did not think about her lesser-skilled students because she never had to think about them. As noted earlier, the traditional PE model either ignores or discourages critical thinking (Blitzer, 1995; McBride, 1995; Williams, 1996; Tishman & Perkins, 1995). It is likely that Mrs. Kirkpatrick's teacher training never required her to think beyond the skills and

24

routines that comprise a traditional PE program. In this particular case, it took a near disaster to lead her to a different path.

Student perceptions of PE

"... PE is about one thing: Being humiliated by your physically superior classmates." Stephen Colbert: The Colbert Report

Looking to better understand the students' perspectives, Smith (1991) posed the question, "Where is the child in physical education research? (p. 37)." He was referring to the lack of meaningful research, up to that point, that included the child's point of view. Smith stresses the need to draw, from child observations, a more inclusive concept of PE and he calls for a human science approach and "child-oriented conceptualization" of how PE can be taught. "[T]here is a methodology at work in our pedagogical inquiries that has less to do with techniques and procedures and more to do with the responsibility we have for children's lives and the empathic understanding through which we can remember the best thing to do for this child at this place and time" (Smith, 1991 p. 47-48). It has been suggested that a greater awareness of students' perceptions and interests could encourage teachers to adapt or modify a program, activity, or teaching approach (Coe, 1984). In other words, PE program modifications should be informed, at least in part, by the PE students. Since students regularly evaluate the teachers' performance and impact, an understanding of student perceptions can help the teacher administer suitable and meaningful educational interventions, as well as improving teaching

25

strategies and curricula (Mergendoller & Packer, 1985; Sanders, 1996; Weiss & Stuntz, 2004).

The views of lower-skilled students in PE should be of particular interest to PE educators because of developmental concerns related to the concept of sociometric status, or the degree of social acceptance among peers. Lee et al. (1995) found that the criteria children use for judging ability changes with age and social development. Young children (kindergarten to grade one) tend to have an unrealistic and egotistical view of their ability and rarely engage in social comparison. As children grow older and more socially aware, however, they begin to judge ability in comparison to their peers.

This social comparison among peers leads to a degree of acceptance, or *sociometric status*, ranging from popular (well liked by peers) to rejected (least liked by peers) (Dunn et al., 2007; Gifford-Smith & Brownell, 2003). Perceived athletic competence appears to be correlated to high sociometric status among children, as reported correlations vary from $r = .44$ to $r = .54$ for sample populations ranging from 46 to 126 (Dunn et al., 2007; Page & Scanlan, 1994; Portman, 2003; Weiss & Duncan, 1992; Weiss & Stuntz, 2004). Therefore, physical competence may be an important factor that either increases or decreases student acceptance by peers (Page & Scanlan, 1994; Weiss & Duncan, 1992). One of the traditional PE practices has been selecting team captains to choose sides for a competition (McCallum, 2000). Students who possess good sports skills (and high sociometric status) tend to be chosen

26

as captains or picked first while students of low skill levels tend to be either chosen last or excluded all together (Evans & Roberts, 1987).

Lesser skilled students, who often receive the brunt of peer criticism and aggression, tend to exhibit humiliation, embarrassment, and frustration in PE class (Carlson, 1995; Portman, 1995; Robinson, 1990; Walling & Martinek, 1995). These negative experiences could lead to increased feelings of sadness, anxiety, depression, isolation, and withdrawal (Dunn et al., 2007; Fitzpatrick & Watkinson, 2003). Such withdrawal increases the "social distance" between these students and their peers (Portman, 2003), and could increase the risk of negative social development (e.g., delinquency, school failure, and psychological maladjustment) (Gifford-Smith & Brownell, 2003).

Students who compare negatively to their peers and fear negative social comparison tend to be less optimistic, avoid participation, and develop negative attitudes towards PE. The practice of competition could lead to a forced social comparison where performance has both negative and positive effects on students' social standing (Ames, 1984). Since children beyond the earlier school grades begin to compare their ability with peers, low-skilled children tend to disassociate themselves from performance and actions that might attract negative attention. They also tend to become easily discouraged; appear indifferent, disinterested, or unmotivated; display difficulty concentrating; and give up quickly (Covington, 1985; Portman, 2003; Robinson, 1990).

27

Learned helplessness

"As an athlete relishes the anticipation of an upcoming competition, and a champion savors a win, the player who is physically awkward is concerned about upcoming forced participation in a game or sport and the anticipated expectation of failure" (Fitzpatrick & Watkinson, 2003, p. 292).

The concept of learned helplessness (Seligman, 1975) may have application in understanding the experience of low-skilled students in PE. Learned helplessness is a perception of futility regardless of what one does, which could lead to a perceived lack of interest in performances and tasks and unwillingness to learn new skills (Martinek & Griffith, 1994; Walling & Martinek, 1995).

The pattern of learned helplessness could look like this

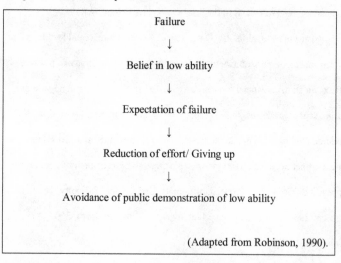

Failure

↓

Belief in low ability

↓

Expectation of failure

↓

Reduction of effort/ Giving up

↓

Avoidance of public demonstration of low ability

(Adapted from Robinson, 1990).

Carlson (1995) studied students alienated from PE and found that these students felt isolation from their peers, considered themselves as low-skilled and lacked personal meaning for physical activity. She identified four extrinsic factors -- (1) teacher personality and behavior, (2) curriculum, (3) class environment, and 4) out of school influences -- and the three intrinsic factors: (1) ability, (2) self-esteem, and (3) student beliefs that contribute to alienation.

Portman suggested that "physical educators lack systematic information about low-skilled students' experiences in physical education and the long term consequences of being low skilled" (Portman, 1995, p.445). In addition, rejection of the student by the teacher may be considered a "key factor" in school failure (Gifford-Smith & Brownell, 2003, p. 248). As a result, it is imperative for teachers to recognize student perceptions in order to establish a genuine, facilitative environment and enable students to maintain optimism and effort without having to compare themselves with others (Lee et al., 1995). It should also be imperative for teachers to be aware of the factors that contribute to peer sociometric status and how PE potentially contributes to both positive and negative social development of both high and low skilled students (Dunn et al., 2007; Page & Scanlan, 1994).

Empathy as an educational tool

Empathy involves an affective mode of understanding, an ability to perceive and share the emotions of another (Davis, 1996; Eisenberg & Strayer, 1987; Hoffman, 1987; Rogers, 1983). Research has shown empathy to be a

29

naturally-occurring human inclination (Kohn, 1990). Studies of newborns have shown natural empathetic reactions to others' distress (Sagi & Hoffman, 1976; Simner, 1971). Studies of toddlers and children have also shown a natural inclination toward empathetic and prosocial behavior (Kohn, 1990, Waxler et al., 1977; Yarrow et al., 1973; Yarrow et al., 1976). Empathy has shown to inhibit aggression and other antisocial behaviors in children (Aspy & Roebuck, 1983; Feshbach & Feshbach, 1969; Miller & Eisenberg, 1988), increase responsibility and helping behavior (Chapman et al, 1987), and increase academic achievement (Feshbach & Feshbach, 1987). Studies have also shown that children with high self-esteem tend to exhibit helping and caring (prosocial) behavior (Kohn, 1990).

Several theorists posit that empathy is a complex multidimensional construct that includes both cognitive and affective capabilities (Davis, 1980, 1983; Eisenberg & Strayer, 1987; Hoffman, 1987). Although empathy is considered to be naturally-occurring in humans, lower-level forms of empathy could be viewed as involuntary distress responses (Kohn, 1990). There is no guarantee that the capacity for higher-level empathy and prosocial behavior will naturally develop in all humans (Davis, 1996; Emde, 1989). Hoffman (1987) described the following developmental levels of empathy: (1) Global empathy – an emotional response to another's distress, e.g., an infant cries when hearing another crying, (2) Egocentric empathy – awareness of another's distress yet without the ability to feel beyond the self, (3) Empathy for another's feelings – an increased awareness of another's distress different than the self produces a more responsive reaction toward the other, and (4) Empathy for another's condition – a more thorough capacity to feel for not only another person, but an entire group of people. This level can lead to acts of prosocial behavior and provide a foundation to moral development (Hoffman, 2000; Huitt, 2005).

Studies conducted on empathy suggest that the capacity to take the perspective of others (higher-order empathy) is a developmentally acquired ability (Davis, 1983; Hatcher et al., 1994; Hoffman, 1987; Kegan, 1982; Kohlberg, 1981; Kohn, 1990; Okeefe & Johnston 1989). Results of studies by Kalliopuska and Roukonen (1993) and Hatcher et al. (1994) suggest that naturally occurring empathy can be enhanced by an educational program. With that in mind, improvements can be made in teaching future teachers to understand the needs of all of their students. Interactive relationships between teacher and student play an important role in the formation of student attitudes, motivation, comfort level, and success in PE (Aicinena, 1991; Bekiari et al., 2005; Cothran, 2001; Koka & Hein, 2006; Stelzer, 2005). Teachers who work on knowing and understanding students in order to gauge their perceptions and abilities will more likely have success than teachers who do not. On the contrary, research shows that highly competitive individuals exhibit decreased levels of empathy (Barnet & Bryan, 1974; Barnett, Matthews, Corbin 1979; Barnett, Matthews, Howard, 1979; Kohn, 1986) and that the current generation of college students is more self-centered and narcissistic than previous

31

generations (Twenge, 2006). Therefore, there appears to be a need to specifically focus on affective development in teacher education.

For the purposes of this study, the definition of empathy offered by Hoffman (1987) will be applied. Hoffman defines empathy as "an affective response more appropriate to someone else's situation than one's own" (p. 48). In order to better facilitate those who have experienced difficulty or failure in PE, it will be necessary for PE teachers to relate to students with physical abilities quite different than their own.

Both Freire and Rogers advocate affective forms of education in an effort to fully emancipate and develop human potential (O'Hara, 1989). Freire (1983) contends that humanization is the educational path toward human emancipation. He stresses that dialogue between the teacher and the student should be rooted in a mutual faith, trust, and humility, with the teacher acting as a facilitator and mutual learner, rather than a dispenser of official information. "Education must begin with the solution of the teacher-student contradiction, by reconciling the poles of the contradiction so that both are simultaneously teachers and students (Freire, 1983, p.72). Rogers (1983) believed in the student's innate capacity for growth and the importance of the relationship between the teacher and student. His person-centered approach emphasizes that learning can occur more readily when the teacher can warmly accept students, provide unconditional positive regard, and empathize with students' feelings (Zimring, 1994). "When the teacher has the ability to understand the student's reactions from the inside, has a sensitive awareness of

32

the way the process of education and learning seems *to the student*, then again, the likelihood of significant learning is increased" (Rogers, 1983, p. 125, italics in original).

Rogers advocated three central concepts for humanistic education:

1. The teacher is congruent or integrated with the student. The teacher is genuine.

2. The teacher demonstrates unconditional positive regard for the student.

3. The teacher experiences an empathic understanding of the student's point of view (Rogers, 1983, Zimring, 1994).

Both Rogers and Freire promote education as a student-centered, humanizing endeavor that requires the teacher to be conscious of students' perceptions, needs, and capabilities. While advocating a departure from the traditional forms of education that often dehumanize and discourage students, both stress education through dialogue, understanding, caring, and a sense of possibility (O'Hara, 1989).

In regards to PE, evidence has been presented that decreased levels of physical activity in students may be attributed to lack of interest (Carlson, 1995; Tinning & Fitzclarence, 1992), negative perceptions (Stork & Sanders, 1996; Wescott, 1992), poor social status (Dunn et al., 2007; Evans & Roberts, 1987; Fitzpartick & Watkinson, 2003; Gifford-Smith & Brownell, 2003), and learned helplessness (Robinson, 1990; Walling & Martinek, 1995). It is

33

conceivable that PE teachers can influence how students are accepted by peers in their classes (Dunn et al., 2007; Weiss & Stuntz, 2004). At the very least, PE teachers can influence how students perceive themselves. Empathic awareness may help teachers to identify such feelings and work on ways to accommodate students' emotional needs. PE should not limit itself solely to physical development (AAHPERD, 1999). Attention must be given to the social and psychological psyches of students – what it feels like to be them. Participation in physical activity and play generates deep feelings, and acknowledgement and appreciation of such emotions can considerably add to enjoyment and understanding of one's involvement in the activity (Laker, 2000).

The relation of the principal literature to the study

As the forgoing discussion indicates, the proposed study builds upon and extends several key themes in the relevant literature. To summarize the main points of that longer discussion, school PE provides the best potential venue for addressing and improving lifelong physical activity among students (DeCorby et al., 2005; Janzen, 2003/2004; Siedentop & Locke, 1997), which is essential for a healthy mind and body (Satcher, 2005; Sosa, 1995; Symons et al., 1997; USDHHS, 2000). Traditional PE, however, creates an unbalanced educational situation that benefits few while alienating students who are not physically gifted or who have not had the opportunities to develop the gifts they may have (Carlson, 1995; Grineski & Bynum, 1996; Portman, 2003; Stevens-Smith, 2002; Villaire, 2001; Virshup, 1999; Westcott, 1992). This

34

situation of decreasing student health created by decreasing levels of physical activity necessitates a change from traditional PE practices and requires not only increased attention to the subject area but also to a change in thinking about how classes can benefit everyone (Blitzer, 1995; Corbin, 2002; Grineski, 1992; Locke, 1992; Tishman & Perkins, 1995; Williams, 1994). Numerous writers and reformers have postulated that affective characteristics and practices are essential for meaningful teaching and lifelong learning (Aspy & Roebuck, 1977; Darling-Hammond & Sykes, 2003; Noddings, 1992; Rogers, 1983). But there is an absence of empirical research both (1) as to how to institute such practices in the PE class and (2) as to the effectiveness of such efforts. The proposed study expands upon prior efforts (1) by introducing a sharper focus on affective development in PE teacher education, with particular attention given to empathetic practice, (2) by assessing student outcomes of an affective-oriented PE teacher education program for aspiring PE educators, and (3) expanding upon existing empathy studies in other areas of education such as music education (Kalliopuska & Roukonen, 1993), counseling education (Cutcliffe & Cassedy, 1999; Hatcher et al., 1994), and cultural studies (Cruz & Patterson, 2005; Goodman, 2000; McAllister & Irvine, 2002).

Research questions

This study has proposed that participant empathy levels, as measured by the Davis Interpersonal Reactivity Index (IRI) (Davis, 1080) will improve following a semester-long college-level physical education methods course

35

with specifically focused lessons and activities on empathy and affective development.

1. In pre-service PE teachers, do experimental and control groups' empathy levels differ, after initial differences are accounted for?

2. For pre-service PE teachers, do experimental and control groups' personal views of PE differ in pre-post effects on empathy, recognition of ability differences, and/or increased intention to help others?

CHAPTER 3: METHODOLOGY

Overall design

This study investigated the effects of an empathy-based teaching approach in a semester-long college-level physical education methods class. Participants in the experimental groups were exposed to specific lessons and activities that stressed affective development and the use of empathetic practice as a teaching strategy. A quantitative pre-post quasi-experimental design with a control group was used to measure changes in pre-existing empathy levels among participants. Quantitative measurement was obtained with the use of the IRI scale. Additionally, qualitative data were obtained from subject essay responses to the following prompt: "Choose four descriptive words you hope your students would use to describe you as a teacher."

Participants

Participants in this study were 59 pre-service teachers (male and female) studying in Physical Education Teacher Education programs in three east-coast universities located in the east/north east of the U.S. These subjects were affiliated as follows:

1. Eighteen students from University 1: Experimental group 1

2. Fifteen students from University 2: Experimental Group 2

3. Twenty six students from University 3: Control groups 1 & 2

37

Characteristics of the study population

Having completed their general education requirements, subjects were working on core courses at the sophomore to senior level of their studies; many of them preparing to student teach within the next few semesters. All participants were enrolled in a Methods of Teaching Elementary Physical Education course. Although students in the experimental groups were required to attend classes and participated in empathy awareness activities, they were under no obligation to participate in further data-gathering activities, nor was such participation graded.

Participant groupings

Experimental group 1: The first experimental group (E1) consisted of 18 University 1 students enrolled in *Methods of Teaching Physical Education in the Elementary Schools*. This is a core course required for teacher education students by the Physical Education Teacher Education (PETE) program. Course description: *Class will focus on the various methods, activities, equipment, and techniques of teaching elementary school physical education. In-class activities will be conducted with both peer instruction or visiting groups of elementary school students. Off-campus teaching experiences will take place in participating elementary schools* (University 1 course catalogue).

Experimental group 2: The second experimental group (E2) consisted of 15 University 2 students enrolled in *Teaching Elementary School Activities*. This is a required course for degree completion of the Physical Education Certification program and State teaching certification.

Course description: *A course in physical education pedagogy emphasizing the varied teaching methods and materials in individual and group activities and games appropriate for the preschool and elementary school: fundamental movement concepts and skills, moving with small equipment, educational games and sports lead-ups, skill themes, educational gymnastics. In-class activities will be conducted with instruction to visiting groups of elementary school students* (University 2 course catalogue).

The two control groups consisted of students enrolled in two courses at University 3. Both courses are required for degree completion in the Physical Education Certification program and State teaching certification.

Control group 1: The first control group (C1) consisted of 15 students enrolled in *Methods and Materials of Teaching Elementary Level Physical Education.*

Course description: *This course is designed to provide preservice elementary physical education teachers opportunities to learn, experience, and apply different teaching styles, teaching skills, strategies, and the knowledge base needed to become an effective physical education teacher. Topics will include: student characteristics, including growth and development; pedagogical strategies; strategies for impacting student learning, including organization management, and teaching styles implications, student and teacher*

39

assessment; strategies for working with special needs populations; and game

model. Students are required to participate in an internship experience in a

local elementary school (University 3 course catalogue).

Control group 2: The second control group (C2) consisted of 11 students

enrolled in *Preschool and Elementary Physical Education Content.*

Course description: *This course is designed to help pre-service physical*

education teachers acquire the knowledge, skills, and attitudes necessary to

effectively teach physical education at the elementary level. Topics will

include: curriculum and lesson planning, assessment, skill themes,

instructional approaches, content development, safety considerations, class

management and organization, and behavior and management strategies.

Students will have the opportunity to practice teaching basic skill themes,

games & sports, aquatics, gymnastics, and fitness activities. Students are

required to participate in an internship experience in a local elementary

school (University 3 course catalogue).

Instrument (Dependent variable)

The dependent variable in this study was empathy as measured by the

Interpersonal Reactivity Index (IRI) (Davis, 1980), which was administered to

subjects in all groups both at the beginning and end of the Spring, 2009

Semester. The IRI is a 28-item survey designed to measure individual

differences of empathy based on a multidimensional approach that addresses both cognitive and affective empathic qualities (Davis, 1980, 1983, 1996). The survey items are scored on a 5-point Likert-type scale ranging from 0 (*does not describe me very well* to 4 (*describes me very well*). One third of the questions are scored in reverse.

Davis (1980) developed the scale to measure a multi-faceted concept of empathy in light of the fact that previous empathy scales produced only a single empathy score. "Rather than treating empathy as a single unipolar construct...the rationale underlying the IRI is that empathy can best be considered as a set of constructs, related in that they all concern responsivity to others but are also clearly discriminable from each other" (Davis, 1983, p. 113). The IRI consists of four 7-item subscales, each designed to measure specific cognitive and affective empathic qualities including: the Empathic Concern (EC) scale, the Fantasy (FS) scale, the Perspective-Taking (PT) scale, and the Personal Distress (PD) scale. Survey items are randomized, with each item scored on a scale of 0 to 4 as described above (Davis, 1980).

The internal consistency reliability of the IRI has been reported to range from .71 to .79 for the four subscale measures while the test-retest reliability ranged from .61 to .81 over an eight to ten week period (Davis, 1980). Davis (1983) reported convergent and discriminant validity of the IRI subscales in a study involving the administration of several psychological tests and questionnaires to 1,344 college students enrolled in an introduction to psychology class. Davis (1983) tested the relationship of the subscales with other potentially related constructs (social competence/ interpersonal

41

functioning, self-esteem, emotionality, sensitivity to others, and intelligence) as well as other highly used psychological measures. He found that that the IRI subscales correlated with expected direction and distinctive aspects of global empathy. Specifically, the EC subscale was related to external measures of emotionality such as selflessness and concern for others, the PT subscale was positively related to measures of interpersonal functioning (extraversion) such as higher social functioning and higher self-esteem, negatively related to measures of dysfunction, and unrelated to measures of emotionality, the FS scale was unrelated to measures of self-esteem or social functioning but moderately related to measures of verbal intelligence; and finally, the PD scale was strongly related to lower self-esteem, poor interpersonal functioning, emotional vulnerability, uncertainty and fearfulness. The examination of intercorrelations between the IRI subscales revealed that the EC scale was significantly and positively related to the PT scale (mean $r = .33$), PT was consistently and negatively related to the PD scale (mean $r = -.25$), and EC and FS were positively correlated (mean $r = .33$). Other non-significant intercorrelations included FS – PT (mean $r = .13$, FS – PD (mean $r = .07$), and EC – PD (mean $r = .08$). Davis (1980) concluded that the IRI subscales displayed predicted relationships among themselves as well as with other empathy measures, which provide "considerable evidence for a multidimensional approach to empathy"(p. 113).

The IRI subscales align in association with Hoffman's (1987) theory on empathy as a developmental progression of stages (Davis, 1980). In this

42

sequence, PD represents "egocentric empathy," FS represents "emerging empathy for another's feelings" through association with fictional characters, EC represents affective empathy, and PT represents cognitive empathy. EC and PT in conjunction form the basis of role playing, which is necessary for higher empathic function such as "empathy for another's life condition" (Hoffman, 1987).

Since the IRI has been widely used, many scoring variations have been devised including employment of a single overall score, selective subscale measurement, combining subscales, eliminating survey items, and so forth (Pulos et al., 2004). Further descriptions of the IRI subscales and an additional measurement of interest (ECPT) are as follows:

Empathic Concern (EC): This scale represents the tendency of the participant to express feelings of warmth and compassion toward others (Davis, 1980) and assess "other-oriented feelings of sympathy and concern for unfortunate others" (Davis, 1983, p. 114).

Fantasy Scale (FS): This scale represents the ability of the participant to identify with fictitious characters in stories, books, or film (Davis, 1980), and the "tendencies to transpose themselves imaginatively into the feelings and actions of fictitious characters" (Davis, 1983, p. 114).

Perspective Taking (PT): This represents the cognitive dimension of empathy, the ability to "anticipate the behavior and reactions of others" (Davis, 1983, p. 115). Davis also expects high PT scores to be associated with higher social

43

functioning and high self-esteem. While PT measures cognitive empathy, the other three (EC, FS, PD) subscales are designed to measure affective components of empathy (Hatcher et al., 1994).

Personal Distress (PD): This scale represents the participant's discomfort when "witnessing the negative experiences of others" (Davis, 1980, p. 6). This scale measures "self-oriented feelings of personal anxiety and unease in tense interpersonal settings" (Davis, 1983, p. 114). Higher PD scores tend to be related to lower self-esteem and poor interpersonal functioning. Davis suggested that the PD subscale be measured separately from the other subscales because of a negative correlation with the higher-order forms of empathy (EC & PT). PD tends to decrease with age "as it measures an early and egocentric precursor of true empathy" (Hatcher et al., 1994), while the other three subscales (FS, EC, & PT) were shown to increase with age maturity (Davis, 1980, Hatcher et al., 1994).

Higher-Order Empathy score: (ECPT): This composite score represents higher-order empathy, combining the affective and cognitive empathy IRI subscales respectively (Davis, 1980). Davis considered EC and PT to develop hand-in-hand, as he reported that "greater perspective-taking ability is associated with greater feelings of empathic concern for others" (p. 17).

Intervention (Independent variable)

The independent variable, administered to the two experimental groups, consisted of lessons and activities designed to facilitate and develop humanistic education strategies and empathic understanding of public perceptions of PE, student perceptions of PE, increased awareness and understanding of the concepts of sociometric status and learned helplessness, the benefits of caring and helping behaviors, and the potential of PE to lead the way toward a healthy society. These lessons were embedded in the regular curricula of the two experimental group methods classes and were subjects of class discussions. Some lessons were included in reflection writing assignments, tests, and class papers. Lessons were designed by the two course instructors and included the following readings and activities:

1. Williams, N. F. (1992). The Physical education hall of shame. *Journal of Physical Education, Recreation and Dance*, 63, 57-60. This article identifies several traditional PE activities that are considered not in the best interest of all students and focuses on improving PE with developmentally appropriate activities beneficial for all.

2. Williams, N. F. (1994). The Physical education hall of shame part II. *Journal of Physical Education, Recreation and Dance*, 65, 17-20. This article continues identification of inappropriate PE activities and urges professionals to be accountable for sound, appropriate PE programs.

3. Williams, N. F. (1996). The physical education hall of shame part III Inappropriate teaching practices. *Journal of Physical Education,*

Recreation and Dance, 67, 45-48. This article focuses on poor teaching practices which reflect a lack of critical thinking in teachers preparation and instruction.

4. National Association for Sport and Physical Education (NASPE) Position Statements on developmentally appropriate and inappropriate PE activities. These statements reflect appropriate PE practices, current issues in PE, and other key topics consistent with NASPE's vision of a physically educated society.

5. Duncan, C. A., Nolan, J., & Wood, R. (2002). See you in the movies? We hope not! *Journal of Physical Education, Recreation and Dance*, 73, 38-44. This article reviews the negative portrayal of PE in film, and includes a listing and synopsis of 39 unflattering movie scenes.

6. *Mr. Woodcock*. (2007). Dobkin, D., & Cooper, B. (Producers), Gillespie, C (Director). United States: New Line Cinema. The opening segment of this film provides a dramatic portrayal of the traditional "gym teacher" who displays a lack of empathy for his students and casts dehumanizing humiliation upon them.

7. *Classroom of the heart* (1991). Written by Guy Doud and produced by Focus on the Family, Colorado Springs, CO. This short film features motivational speaker and former National Teacher of the Year, Guy Doud who describes his own painful experiences in school, particularly

his struggle with low self-esteem as a result of negative "gym class" experiences.

8. *No more dodgeball: The new phys. ed in Michigan schools.* (1997). Produced by the Michigan Association for Health, Physical Education, Recreation, and Dance. This short film opens with an anecdotal collection of negative experiences in traditional PE and details efforts to re-invent PE as student-centered, fitness-based class.

9. *Sociometric Status* (Appendix F): This handout, along with accompanying lecture and discussion, outlines sociometric status and the major factors that affect student social status in school.

10. *Learned Helplessness* (Appendix G): This handout, along with accompanying lecture and discussion, outlines the pattern of learned helplessness and the factors that may contribute to it in the PE class.

11. *Carl Rogers: student-centered education* (Appendix H): This handout describes Rogers' three central concepts for humanistic education and the importance of the teacher-student relationship.

Data collection

1. During the first class of the 2009 spring semester, subjects in all groups were invited by the researcher to participate in a research study in the area of teacher education. The basis of the study was explained to them and after all questions were answered, the

47

students were asked to give their consent to participate by signing an IRB-approved informed consent document. All subjects invited chose to participate. The informed consent documents were distributed and collected by an IRB-trained graduate assistant.

2. All subjects were administered the IRI during the first class of the spring, 2009 semester.

3. Surveys were collected by the graduate assistant and coded to assure anonymity, but that allowed matching individual pre and post responses. This matching was accomplished by numbering each survey. The graduate assistant was then given a list of numbers on which to record the subjects' names along with the number. The graduate assistant kept the list in order to re-distribute same names/numbers for the post-test.

4. All subjects were also invited to participate in the essay assignment during the first class of the spring, 2009 semester. All subjects invited chose to participate. Subjects were given 20 minutes to complete a reflective essay in response to: "Choose four descriptive words you hope your students would use to describe you as a teacher." Subjects were directed to not disclose any personal identifying information on the essays.

5. Each essay was sealed in a numbered envelope. The numbers corresponded to the same list of names/numbers as was used for the

48

survey. The assistant kept the list and envelopes in order to re-distribute the essays to the same subjects for the post-essay.

6. The experimental groups participated in the curricular intervention in addition to regular course content during the spring, 2009 semester while the control groups participated in regular course content.

7. On the last day of class of the spring, 2009 semester, all subjects were re-administered the IRI. Each survey was numbered and the assistant matched the numbers with the pre-test names/numbers. Surveys were collected by the graduate assistant. The assistant gave numbered surveys (pre and post) to the investigator.

8. On the last day of the spring, 2009 semester, all subjects were also asked to participate in the essay assignment. After the second essay was completed, the graduate assistant gave each subject his/her numbered envelope containing the first writing. A second essay prompt: "Read your essay from the beginning of the semester and compare it to the one you just wrote. Reflect upon similarities or differences between the two. What things changed?" was administered. Subjects were instructed to write the reflection after comparing their two written essays. Students were given 20 -30 minutes to complete the essay and reflection.

9. Essays were sealed in numbered envelopes and collected by the graduate assistant. The assistant gave the envelopes to the investigator without revealing the list of names.

Quantitative Analysis

Descriptive statistics were calculated for each individual IRI subscale (EC, FS, PT, PD), and the composite higher-order empathy score ECPT (EC + PT subscales). In order to conserve statistical power, three of the above scores were chosen for further analysis: ECPT, and remaining subscales FS and PD. An ANCOVA (pre/post experimental/ control) was utilized to look for differences over time between the groups while controlling for pre-test differences.

Justification for the use of an ECPT measurement was based on the following factors: First, EC and PT are representative of affective and cognitive empathy respectively. The findings of several prior studies have suggested that the EC and PT subscales represent the strongest and most central empathy components (Alterman et al., 2003, Siu & Shek, 2005). Alterman et al. (2003) conducted a confirmatory factor analysis on a three-factor IRI model (FS, PD, and EC + PT composite labeled *Empathy factor*). Analysis revealed that structure loading of all components of Empathy factor were over .40, ranging from .51 to .73. Internal consistency was reported with alpha coefficients for Empathy factor (.82), FS (.72), and PD (.69). Correlations with the other two IRI scales demonstrated Empathy factor as

50

"relatively independent" of the FS (.34) and PD (.09) scales (Alterman et al., 2003, p. 262).

Collectively, EC + PT represent the empathic response. For a person to be "fully empathic," he or she must respond to a particular stimulus with both a "cognitive/intellectual ability" to recognize the portrayed emotion and an "emotional reaction to the stimulus" (Davis, 1980, p. 4). A composite score of the EC and PT subscales has been used by other researchers and centrally labeled such as, "The Empathy Scale (ES)" (Siu & Shek, 2005, p. 122) and Empathy factor" (Alterman et al., 2003, p. 263). Siu & Shek (2005) considered EC and PT subscales to be "representative of the empathic response," while PD and FS were considered to be "antecedents and consequences of empathy" (p. 120).

Secondly, the EC and PT subscales go hand-in-hand as both are expected to increase with maturity at the same basic rate (Davis, 1980). Thirdly, after analyzing the hierarchical structure of the IRI, Pulos et al. (2004) suggested that a higher-order empathy scale could be derived from a "simple sum" of the EC, FS, and PT subscales (p. 359). However, Hatcher's results suggested that a FS increase takes place more apparently during adolescent (high school) years while EC and PT better develop during the college years, which parallel development of abstract thought, advanced morals, and introspection. A focus on a higher-order scale comprising of EC and PT may better serve a college-level study. Finally, while the IRI is based on Hoffman's theory of developmental empathy, ECPT represents Hoffman's (1987) advanced

51

developmental empathy levels which he considered to be the basis of moral

development and the foundation of altruistic behavior (Hoffman, 2000).

Results of previous studies have shown strong EC and PT dispositions to be

predictors of altruistic behaviors (Davis, 1983; Espelage et al, 2003; Litvack-

Miller, 1997; Osswald, 2003). Higher forms of empathy are also considered

important predispositions toward perceiving concern for others – a necessary

component of democratic education (Hunt, 2007; Morrell, 2003). Since higher

forms of empathy appear to be congruent with caring, helping, moral

judgment, and justice - all of which are desirable qualities for a teacher to

have, further examination of ECPT appears applicable to a study involving

preservice teachers.

In sum, although the four subscales of the IRI are considered to be

representative of distinct aspects of empathy, some researchers consider EC

and PT to be the basis of empathic response (Alterman et al., 2003; Espelage et

al, 2003; Siu & Shek, 2005). Analysis of ECPT as a composite score allows

the researcher the opportunity to observe what some researchers consider the

interactive contributions of desired affective and cognitive dimensions of

empathy during the college years, the optimal age for its development.

Qualitative analysis

In addition to the administration of the IRI, students were asked to write an

essay directing the student to "Choose four descriptive words you hope your

students would use to describe you as a teacher." Students were given a hand-

52

out and asked to write the essay. At the end of the spring, 2009 semester students were asked to repeat the same essay assignment. Upon completion, they were given the envelope containing their first essay. Students were then asked to write the following reflection comparing the two essays, "Read your essay from the beginning of the semester and compare it to the one you just wrote. Reflect upon similarities or differences between the two. What things changed? What things stayed the same?" Essays were sealed in a coded envelope and collected by the graduate assistant. All identifiers were removed to assure anonymity. Essays were analyzed using a pre-post content analysis.

CHAPTER 4: RESULTS

The purpose of this research study was to determine the effect of a semester-long empathy-focused educational intervention on empathy levels in pre-service teachers studying in PE Teacher Education. In line with this, two research questions were formulated:

1. In pre-service PE teachers, do experimental and control groups' empathy levels differ, after initial differences are accounted for?

2. For pre-service PE teachers, do experimental and control groups' personal views of PE differ in pre-post effects on empathy, recognition of ability differences, and/or increased intention to help others?

To answer the two research question the following hypotheses were formulated:

H_{o1}: There will be no difference between the empathy levels of pre-service PE teachers following a semester-long college-level PE methods course with specifically focused empathy and affective activities and the empathy levels of pre-service PE teachers following a semester-long college-level PE methods course without this specific content.

H_{a1}: Empathy levels of pre-service PE teachers following a semester-long college-level PE methods course with specifically focused empathy and affective development activities will be greater than the

54

empathy levels of pre-service PE teachers following a semester-long college-level PE methods course without this specific content. .

H_{o2}: There will be no difference between pre-service teachers' reflections of their personal views of PE following a semester-long college-level PE methods course with specifically focused empathy and affective development activities and the personal views of PE preservice teachers following a semester-long college-level PE methods course without this specific content.

H_{a2}: Pre-service PE teachers' personal view of PE following a semester-long college-level PE methods course with specifically focused empathy and affective development activities will show greater empathy, recognition of ability differences, and/or increased intention to help others than the personal views of pre-service PE teachers following a semester-long college-level PE methods course without this specific content.

The first research question was addressed through quantitative data and analysis. The second research question was addressed through qualitative data and analysis. To test hypothesis one, descriptive statistics were analyzed and presented for each individual IRI subscale, the ESUM3 score and the composite ECPT. Although further analysis could have proceeded with the four subscales and the two composite scores, concern for the cumulative Type I error rate suggested limiting the number of inferential tests conducted on essentially the same data. With the intent of retaining the most information from the IRI, in the most meaning forms, the composite ECPT and remaining FS and PD subscale scores were evaluated to look for differences over time between treatment (experiment and control) with pretest subscales as covariate. The analysis of covariance (ANCOVA) procedure was chosen to ensure statistical control of the pre-test difference of the control and experimental group scores on the IRI scale. In addition, since subjects were not randomly assigned to groups the ANCOVA partially adjusts for any preexisting differences among the groups (Hinkle et al., 1998). The study variables are described as the following and the statistical data analysis pertaining hypothesis one is presented thereafter.

Data Screening

After all surveys were collected, each was checked for completion by the researcher. Three surveys were determined to be incomplete and/or unusable and were excluded from the set. The IRI answer sheets for these three subjects presented a distinct graphical pattern which was determined to be unrelated to the survey items. The compiled data was entered into SPSS (version 17.0 for Windows) for calculations, analysis, and report preparations.

Characteristics of the study sample

Participants in this study were 59 pre-service teachers (male and female) studying in PETE Programs at three East-coast universities. Students from two universities made up the experimental groups including 18 students from

University 1 and 15 students from University 2. The control group consisted of 26 students from University 3. Subject demographic information is displayed in Table 1.1. Information on the participating university departments and their students is presented in Table 1.2.

Table 1.1

Descriptive statistics for subject demographic and interest variables.

	Control		Experimental	
N	26		33	
Gender (n and %)	Male, 19 – 73%	Female, 7 - 27%	Male, 23 - 70%	Female, 10 - 30%
Age (years)	X = 21.6 s.d. = 2.6		X = 22.1 s.d. = 2.6	
College Year (n and %)	Sophomore Junior Senior 5+	2 8% 13 50% 8 31% 3 12%	Sophomore Junior Senior 5+	1 3% 12 36% 12 36% 8 24%
Ethnicity (n and %)	Caucasian Af. Am. Hispanic Asian Am. Missing	21 81% 1 4% 1 4% 1 4% 2 8%	Caucasian Native Am. Hispanic	31 94% 1 3% 1 3%
Do you consider yourself to be an athletic	Yes = 26 No = 0		Yes = 33 No = 0	

57

person?		
Is this course required or optional?	Required = 26 Optional = 0	Required = 33 Optional = 0

Table 1.2

Descriptive data for participating university departments.

University	Student population		Dept. faculty (FTEs)	PETE students
	Undergrad.	Grad.		
Experimental 1	12,800	2,300	12	80
Experimental 2	6,000	367	11 + 40 adjunct	222
Control	7,600	3,000	11	85

IRI results

Subject responses to the IRI survey were scored according to established procedures (Davis, 1980). Scores on the four IRI subscales, EC, FS, PT, and PD were calculated along with the ECPT composite score. Descriptive statistics for these results are presented in Table 2. All of the study variables were normally distributed with skewness values falling within the acceptable range of -1 to +1. Therefore, ANCOVA method pertaining to those variables was considered appropriate.

Table 2

Descriptive statistics for dependent variables across independent variable

Subscale	Total (n= 56) mean (s.d.) Skewness	Pre-test (n= 56)		Post-test (n= 52)	
		Control n = 23	Exp. n = 33	Control n = 20	Exp. n = 32
		mean (s.d.) Skewness	mean (s.d.) Skewness	mean (s.d.) Skewness	mean (s.d.) Skewness
EC	19.07 (4.27) -.846	19.35 (4.16) -.52	18.88 (4.40) - 1.51	18.45 (4.01) .72	20.13 (3.71) - .40
FS	16.37 (3.79) .189	15.52 (4.16) .58	16.97 (3.47) .01	14.35 (4.91) - .98	16.19 (3.75) .47
PT	17.50 (4.24) -.20	17.65 (4.31) -.004	17.39 (4.26) - .35	17.55 (3.72) - .34	19.25 (3.75) .10
PD	9.11 (4.16) 1.07	9.09 (2.97) .05	9.12 (4.88) 1.16	9.45 (3.76) - .35	8.59 (3.83) .55
ECPT	36.57 (7.63) -.47	37.00 (7.95) .31	36.27 (7.51) -1.12	36.00 (6.67) .37	39.38 (6.21) - .26

Internal consistency reliability was measured with Cronbach's alpha to assess subscale reliability over time. These values indicate moderate reliability and correspond with Davis' (1980) established test-retest reliability range of .61 to .81.

Table 3

Subscale test-retest reliability

Subscale	EC	FS	PT	PD
Alpha	.74	.75	.64	.57

Analysis of Research Question One

To test research hypothesis one, an ANCOVA was conducted. The post-test IRI subscale scores were the dependent variable, the treatment (experimental group and control group) was the independent variable and the pre-test IRI subscale scores were the covariate. Three separate ANCOVAs were calculated with the dependent variable of empathy defined as 1) ECPT (composite score of EC and PT), 2) subscale FS and 3) subscale PD. Limiting the number of inferential tests and conducting the tests on non-overlapping data allowed for setting the alpha level at .05 for each test. The ANCOVA results are presented in Table 4.

Table 4

ANCOVA tests between subject effects

Source	Sum of Squares	Df	Mean Square	F	Significance
ECPT (covariate)	590.188	1	590.188	19.95	.00**
ECPTp	128.863	1	128.863	4.36	.04*
Error	1449.312	49	29.578		
FS	312.800	1	312.800	26.307	.000**
FSp	9.740	1	9.740	.819	.370
Error	582.625	49	11.890		
PD	111.208	1	111.208	8.883	.004**
PDp	4.701	1	4.701	.375	.543
Error	2114.305	49	43.149		

COVARIATES: ECPT = Higher-Order Empathy pre-test score, FS = Fantasy scale pre-test score, PD = Personal distress pre-test score. BETWEEN GROUP EFFECTS: ECPTp = Higher-Order Empathy post-test score, FSp = Fantasy scale post-test score, PDp = Personal distress post-test score

*, ** significance levels .05, .01 respectively

   Summarizing the quantitative analysis, for the composite score ECPT and

accounting for the pre-test differences in empathy levels in pre-service PE

teachers in the experimental group were significantly higher than in the control

group. The pretest empathy levels explained a large proportion of total

variation in corresponding posttest empathy levels. There was no significant

difference for the comparison based on the IRI FS and PD subscales. Based on

the above results, this study will partially accept hypothesis H_{a1} that the participant empathy levels in pre-service PE teachers improves following a semester-long college-level physical education methods course.

Analysis of Research Question Two

The second hypothesis of this study is that pre-service PE teachers' personal view of PE following a semester-long college-level PE methods course with specifically focused empathy and affective development activities will show greater empathy, recognition of ability differences, and/or increased intention to help others than the personal views of pre-service PE teachers participating in a similar course without this empathy-focused content. Qualitative data were gathered from subjects' reflective essays with prompts as described in the Methods Chapter. All subject essays were transcribed onto a chart which listed subject code, pre-test keywords, post-test keywords and subject's reflection of changes that occurred over the semester. Responses were reviewed and 83 subject identified keywords were documented.

A review of the teacher quality literature by Mowrer-Reynolds (2008) provided guidance in analyzing the 83 key words. This author found that research on perceptions of quality teachers has typically been organized into two categories of characteristics: professional skills (such as knowledge of content, dedicated to the profession, prepared, organized, etc.), and personal teacher characteristics (such as energetic, caring, funny, respectful, etc.). These categories offered a meaningful and useful distinction to apply to the present data. The nature of this study, however, supported dividing personal teaching characteristics further. In aligning with Hoffman's (1987) suggestion that empathy develops from self-oriented personal distress to other-oriented feeling and perspective taking, the personal characteristics were divided into self-and other-oriented categories. Student-centered characteristics (such as caring, empathetic, helpful, and encouraging) were viewed separately from personal teaching characteristics that are superlative in nature (such as awesome, funny, energetic, interesting) that do not necessarily constitute a humanistic or helping capacity. Based on these conceptualizations, informed by Mower-Reynolds' and Hoffman's work, the following three categories were defined:

1. Professional-oriented qualities included those characteristics that focus on the professional requirements of the teaching profession, knowledge of content, preparation and organizational skills, and effectiveness. Included in this category could be words such as dependable, organized, prepared, and professional.

2. Student-centered (other-oriented) personal qualities included those characteristics that are directly related to facilitation of student understanding, caring and success. Included in this category could be words such as empathetic, caring, respectful, and helping.

3. Instructor-centered (self-oriented) personal qualities included those characteristics that are superlative in nature that do not necessarily constitute a humanistic or helping element. Included in this category could be words such as fun, super, interesting, and awesome.

63

Three researchers (author, major professor, and faculty member with extensive experience in qualitative research) assigned each of the 83 identified keywords into one of the three categories. Inconsistencies were identified for seven words. However, in each case, two of the three researchers chose the same category. Therefore, these words were categorized by majority (2/3) selection.

Subject responses for experimental and control groups were organized and tabulated into the above categories. Pre/ post responses for control group and *experimental group* are presented in Table 5.

Table 5: *Frequency of pre and post keyword responses for both control and experimental groups.*

Professional	Pre		Post		Student-centered	Pre		Post		Instructor-centered	Pre		Post	
n = 22 (27%)	C*	E**	C*	E**	n = 24 (29%)	C*	E**	C*	E**	n = 37 (45%)	C*	E**	C*	E**
Consistent	0	0	1	0	Adaptive	0	0	0	1	Amazing	0	0	0	1
Dedicated	0	1	0	1	Approachable	0	3	0	3	Amusing	0	1	0	0
Dependable	0	1	0	1	Calm	0	1	0	0	Athletic	2	2	1	0
Determined	0	0	0	1	Caring	8	5	5	5	Awesome	0	0	2	1
Effective	3	3	1	3	Compassionate	1	0	0	2	Best	0	0	0	1
Fair	2	2	1	0	Easy to talk to	0	1	0	0	Confident	0	2	0	0
Focused	1	0	0	0	Empathetic	0	2	0	1	Cool	1	0	0	0
Honest	0	0	2	3	Encouraging	1	1	1	1	Creative	6	4	6	0
Informative	0	1	0	1	Good listener	0	1	0	0	Dude	0	0	1	0
Insightful	0	0	0	1	Helpful	4	5	3	3	Emotional	0	0	1	1
Interactive	1	0	0	0	Influential	0	1	0	0	Energetic	3	6	3	4

64

	C*	E**	C*	E**		C*	E**	C*	E**		C*	E**	C*	E**
Knowledgeable	9	6	4	5	Inspiring	2	0	1	1	Enjoyable	1	0	0	0
Leader/Role model	4	3	3	4	Kind	0	1	1	1	Enthusiastic	2	2	3	6
Organized	1	1	1	2	Leave an Impact	0	0	1	0	Exciting	1	0	3	1
Personable	1	0	1	0	Loyal	1	0	1	0	Fit	1	0	0	0
Prepared	0	0	1	0	Meaningful	1	0	0	0	Friendly	2	2	0	0
Polite	0	1	0	0	Mentor	0	0	0	1	Fun/funny	15	23	12	16
Professional	3	3	1	1	Motivational	4	4	1	4	Good	0	0	0	1
Reliable	0	3	0	1	Open minded	0	1	0	1	Good teacher	0	1	0	0
Respectful	0	6	3	4	Positive	0	1	0	1	Greatest	0	1	0	0
Responsible	2	2	0	0	Protective	0	0	1	0	Hard-working	0	0	0	3
Trustworthy	0	6	0	0	Relatable	0	1	0	0	hot dog	0	0	0	1
	27	**39**	**19**	**28**	Thoughtful	0	0	0	1	Imaginative	0	1	0	0
					Understanding	2	4	3	5	Interesting	5	2	4	1
						24	**42**	**18**	**51**	Nice	0	0	1	2
										Not boring	0	0	0	1
										Outgoing	0	1	0	0
										Passionate	0	1	2	3
										Playful	0	0	1	0
										Pusher	0	1	0	0
										Real	0	0	1	0
										The reason why they come	1	0	0	0
										Smart	2	2	3	7
										Spontaneous	1	0	1	0
										Stud	0	0	1	0
										Stupendous	0	0	0	1
										Weird	0	0	1	0
											43	**52**	**47**	**51**

*Control group, **Experimental group

65

Since analysis on all 83 responses was deemed unwieldy, and there was delineation in the frequency of responses after the top five responses, it was determined that the five most frequent keywords was a reasonable number to consider for further analysis. Frequencies for the top five keyword responses are presented in Tables 6-1 through 6-4. These responses for the Control Group will be presented first (Tables 6-1 and 6-2), followed by the Experimental Group (Tables 6-3 and 6-4).

Overall results of all group top five keyword responses concur with Mowrer-Reynolds' findings from the literature that when asked to identify outstanding teacher qualities, pre-service teachers tend to choose personal characteristics over professional skills. The only professional-oriented keyword appearing in the top five responses was "knowledgeable" (Control 1, 2, Experimental 1), while all other top five responses consisted of both student-centered and instructor centered words.

The control group top five keyword results remained similar between pre and post responses with the exception of a 17 percent decrease in "knowledgeable" between pretest and posttest essay responses. These qualitative results appear to parallel the findings of all control group IRI scale results, which revealed no significant change between pre and post survey results.

Table 6-1

Frequency and percentage of top five keyword pre-test responses for the control group (n = 26).

	Response	Number	Response %
1	Fun/ Funny	15	58%
2	Knowledgeable	9	35%
3	Caring	8	31%
4	Creative	6	23%
5	Interesting	5	19%

Table 6-2

Frequency and percentage of top five keyword post-test responses for the control group (n = 23).

	Response	Number	Response %	pre/post diff. (+.-)
1	Fun/ Funny	12	52%	- 6%
2	Creative	6	26%	+ 3%
3	Caring	5	22%	- 9%
4	Interesting	4	17%	- 2%
5	Knowledgeable	4	17%	- 18%

Tables 6-3 and 6-4 show that top five keywords for the experimental group, pre and post, respectively. The largest change of any variable occurred in the experimental group where the student centered characteristic "empathy/

empathetic" increased in prevalence by 28 percent (6% to 34%). In contrast, the characteristic "empathy/ empathetic" did not appear in any control group keyword list. Also, the experimental group instructor-centered characteristic "fun/ funny" decreased by 20 percent (70% to 50%).

Table 6-3

Frequency and percentage of top five keyword pre-test responses for the experimental group (n = 33).

	Response	Number	Response %
1	Fun/ Funny	23	70%
2	Caring	15	45%
3	Knowledgeable	6	18%
5	Energetic	6	18%
5	Respectful	6	18%
5	Trustworthy	6	18%

Table 6-4.

Frequency and percentage of top five keyword post-test responses for the experimental group (n = 32).

	Response	Number	Response %	pre/post diff. (+.-)
1	Fun/ Funny	16	50%	- 20%
2	Caring	15	47%	+ 2%
3	Empathetic	11	34%	+ 28%
4	Smart/Intelligent	7	22%	+ 16%

5	Enthusiastic	6	19%	+ 13%

Analysis next addressed the post-test essays that asked all subjects to reflect their experiences in the course. The instructions to subjects were as follows: "Read your essay from the beginning of the semester and compare it to the one you just wrote. Reflect upon similarities or differences between the two. What things changed? What things stayed the same?" All essays were read and differences and similarities were identified and summarized. Experimental group essay results indicated a shift in thinking away from self-centered personal characteristics and toward a student-centered inclination; this shift was not seen in the control group essays. This appears to concur with the IRI scale results of the experimental group which showed a significant increase in the composite empathy score.

As previously stated, the thematic analysis revealed a disposition toward empathetic practice among the experimental group. Examples of reflections that illustrate this shift follow.

"Empathy was the main difference I noticed. Putting yourself in the students' perspective is the key. Being an affective teacher was the main difference. However, what I noticed is empathy is the most important aspect of being a great teacher."

"I noticed I changed 2 of my words from fun and motivating to empathetic and enthusiastic. I feel as a person I want to make a difference in others and that was my main goal."

"I am more concerned with empathy and understanding different students' situations rather than just being fun and exciting. I am more concerned with my quality of teaching rather than how students perceive me."

"I learned empathy in this class and brought that into my characteristics because I want to put myself in their shoes."

Other essays reflected on subjects' growth as a person and teacher, and although empathy and closely related words are not used, the underlying themes suggest a disposition related to facilitation of student understanding, caring and success:

"The main difference between the beginning and end of the semester was that at the beginning of the semester my descriptive words were based on what I thought a book would want a teacher to be. After this semester, not just this class, I feel like I have grown up as a person and as a teacher and found what "I" wanted to be rather than what a book tells me to be."

One experimental group subject expressed an increase of instructor-centered characteristics in post test responses:

"My words the second time [were] more praising rather than words that would describe what a good teacher does. The only one that was the same was 'fun'."

Control group essay reflections were noticeably less expressive. In fact, the most common control group reflection was "no change" or "everything stayed the same" (65%). Some selected responses expressed this attitude further:

"I did not change my characteristic. My intentions/ purpose for teaching are and will always remain the same."

"My thought process has not changed about how I want my students to view me."

Still, two of the 23 control group subjects reflected an affirmation toward a caring approach:

"The first sets of answers were more personal and were views that I wanted students to have of me. In contrast, the second sets of answers were more

71

extensive, and how I wanted to feel towards others. I wanted to be more caring
and understanding"

"I would continue to be helpful and as encouraging as possible. I feel this is
vital to one's future. If you are "brought down" at a young age, that will carry
with you throughout your life."

To more fully understand the differences between the experiences of
subjects in the control and experimental groups, a follow-up interview was
conducted with the instructor of the control group courses, who was not aware
of the specific topic of the experiment. A transcript of this interview is
provided in Appendix I. In that interview, the instructor revealed that his
classes were closely tied to the textbook chapters. Other than Hellison's model
of teaching personal social responsibility, and a lesson on motivation, no social
or psychological constructs were introduced or explored in the control classes.

In summary, the qualitative analysis suggested a change in experimental
group subjects' personal view of PE. This was seen in analysis of both the
keyword descriptors and the reflective follow-up essays. The differences were
noted between both the experimental and control groups and between pre and
post experimental group essays. Subjects in the experimental group
demonstrated an increase of empathy and inclination to help others while
decreasing instructor-centered personal characteristics.

Subject reflections further demonstrated a specific change in thinking toward empathy and putting themselves in their students' shoes. This analysis supports the findings of the IRI scale and appears to support hypothesis H_{a2}: that pre-service teachers' reflections of their personal view of PE in pre-post effects on empathy, recognition of ability differences, and/or increased intention to help others significantly improve better in experimental group than control group.

CHAPTER 5: DISCUSSION

Concerns over a sharp decline in physical fitness in the United States have prompted the USDHHS (2000) to call on public education to identify and address barriers that inhibit health and wellness among citizens. PE, with its propensity for physical activity is the most suitable school subject to address this problem. However, evidence suggests that generations of students have been "turned off" to lifelong physical activity because of a myriad of negative experiences in traditional PE (Grineski & Bynum, 1996; Portman, 2003; Villaire, 2001; Westcott, 1992). Because PE teaching candidates tend to come from athletic backgrounds, their success in sport and competition potentially blinds them from the feelings of those of lesser physical abilities (Barnet & Bryan, 1974; Barnett, Matthews, Corbin 1979; Barnett, Matthews, Howard, 1979; Kohn, 1986). In conjunction with current efforts to improve curriculum and assessment, there appears to be a need to improve teaching practice, specifically the development and practice of empathy in order to understand and accommodate a diversity of ability in their future classes. Such action could potentially foster more productive relationships with all PE students, which could lead to greater acceptance of physical activity and ultimately, a more physically fit society.

This study sought to determine if pre-service teachers studying in PE Teacher Education could increase empathy levels through the investigation of a semester-long educational intervention. A quantitative pre-post quasi-experimental design with control groups was used to measure changes in pre-

74

existing empathy levels among participants. The dependent variable was the 28 – item Davis Interpersonal Reactivity Index (IRI), a Likert-type scale that consisting of four subscales, EC, FS,PT, and PD, each designed to measure specific cognitive and affective empathic qualities. An additional qualitative measurement was employed through the pre/post completion of a reflective keyword identification task and an essay. The following section will discuss quantitative and qualitative findings, possible explanations for the results, comparison with other studies, study strengths and limitations, study implications, and suggestions for further research and practice.

Quantitative effects

Results of the pre/post IRI scale indicate a significant difference between experimental and control groups in ECPT, the higher-order empathy scores, following a semester-long educational intervention. These findings suggest that preservice teachers studying PE are able to further develop naturally occurring empathy through participation in a specifically-designed educational program. The significant improvement of higher-order empathy in the experimental group supports similar findings in studies of empathy education reported by Cutcliffe & Cassedy (1999), Hatcher et al. (1994), and Kalliopuska & Roukonen (1993). Improvement of the higher-order empathy scores among experimental groups also concur with the notion that the more advanced cognitive and affective (higher-order empathy), represented by ECPT, is most effectively developed with training during the college years (Hatcher et al., 1994; Hoffman, 1987).

An important aspect of this study was the use of a control group with which to compare experimental group results. The use of a control group was a particular strength of the study as it allowed for differentiating what was learned with an intervention and what was learned through natural development. Since various theories describe empathy as "developmental" and changing over time (Davis, 1983; Davis & Franzoi, 1991; Hatcher et al., 1994; Hoffman, 1987; Kegan, 1982; Kohlberg, 1981; Kohn, 1990), there existed the possibility that subjects would simply develop natural-occurring empathy through maturity, thus threatening internal validity.

Control group subjects in this study participated in regular course content without the intervention of an empathy-based curriculum. Emerging trends indicated a decline in all mean empathy IRI control group scores from pretest to posttest (noting that the control group PD score increased while a decrease in PD is considered an improvement). The lack of improvement in control group scores demonstrated the notion that empathy does not automatically develop with maturity, but must be nurtured for it to fully evolve (Davis, 1996; Emde, 1989). This concurs with Hatcher's conclusion that a formal educational program "is crucial to developing the skills of empathy" (1994, p. 970).

The results also revealed two IRI subscales (FS and PD) that did not show a significant difference between pre and post-test scores. The FS score, which measures empathy associated through association with fictional characters (Davis, 1980) may not have been influenced enough in the educational methods course. Although some film clips and readings were included in the

76

intervention curriculum, there was no extensive presentation of any fictional characters, thus little opportunity for subjects to experience empathy in this fashion. Future studies looking at this particular subscale could be better served with the incorporation of more fictional literature and film into the intervention curriculum. The PD score, representing Hoffman's early level egocentric empathy (Davis, 1980), may not have shown a significant difference because of the college-age level of the subjects. Since PD is related to low self-esteem and social functioning (Davis, 1983), college students studying to be professional educators might not be the ideal population with which to study personal anxiety at others' distress. However, future studies looking at the PD scale may be better served with a longitudinal study addressing the development of empathy, along with a decline in PD across the span of several years.

Qualitative effects

Analysis of the qualitative data revealed subjects overwhelmingly chose to write about personal characteristics (73%) over professional skill characteristics (27%), which is consistent with Mowrer-Reynolds' (2008) review of literature and subsequent study of pre-service teachers' perceptions of exemplary teachers and confirms her assertion that pre-service teachers consider personal characteristics as "invaluable" in helping students increase self-esteem and self-efficacy. This also corroborates past studies that reveal students' perception of relationships between teacher and student play an

77

important role in the formation of student success in PE (Acinena, 1991; Bekiari et al., 2005; Cothran, 2001; Koka & Hein, 2006; Seltzer, 2005).

Qualitative analysis further demonstrated a dispositional change between experimental group pretest and posttest responses while control group responses remained fairly consistent between the two essays. The most prominent change of any group was the inclusion of the word "empathy" or "empathetic" to the list, consisting of a 28% increase in usage. This appears most likely due to the introduction of the concept of empathy as part of the "Carl Rogers: Student-centered education" lesson in one of the experimental groups. However, that particular lesson took up only one day of the 15-week semester (approximately 30 meetings). This could lead one to infer that a combination of the lesson describing empathy, along with corresponding lessons of the intervention curriculum made an impact on the subjects in the experimental group. Such an assumption is supported by several of the subjects' posttest reflections on the topic. On the other hand, no essay results from control group subjects included the term "empathy" in pre or posttest responses and only one reflected a disposition centered on the word "caring." According to the instructor of the two control groups, subjects were not introduced to the concept of "empathy" in any lesson of the control group classes during the semester. Control group reflections further demonstrated a lack of change between pre and posttest replies, most consisting of a single sentence indicating no change in feelings or attitudes from the initial essay response. This appears to indicate that although the subjects of the control

78

group most likely acquired the knowledge and practices of a semester-long methods course, empathetic teaching practice was not part of that acquired information. This conclusion further reinforces Hatcher's (1994) notion that empathy does not necessarily fully develop without the assistance of an educational program.

The qualitative results from the essay and reflection of both experimental and control groups appeared to parallel the quantitative results of the IRI survey. The significant difference between control and experimental groups ECPT scores (while controlling for pre-empathy level differences) was consistent with qualitative reflections indicating a change in experimental subjects' self-perception towards a more empathetic disposition, little to no change in control group subjects' self-perceptions was observed in this regard.

Implications

This study contributed to the existing research on empathy education by introducing empathy and student-centered education in a PE teacher education setting. Although several studies have been conducted on empathy in education and other professional fields, no previous studies have been conducted in the field of PE. Implications of this first-time endeavor are discussed below.

Implications for PE

In many ways, this study could be considered an initial attempt to help answer the USDHHS (2000) call to address and overcome barriers inhibiting the acquisition and maintenance of healthy lifestyles. The foundation of this study rested on the premise that introduction of the concept of empathic teaching practice into preservice PE teacher educators may help future PE teachers recognize and eliminate historical shortcomings, and broaden their understanding of a diversity of ability in their future classes, and shift focus of instructional attention to the physical, social, and emotional needs of all students. Although some fitness-related school PE programs are beginning to emerge, many programs still champion the traditional model, meaning lesser skilled students will likely fail, leading to avoidance of physical activity (Covington, 1985; Fitzpatrick & Watkinson, 2003; Portman, 2003). The most likely juncture to offer a solution is at the teacher education level.

Cultivating empathy in our pre-service teachers involves bringing to light other peoples' (both historical and current) perception of PE, while temporarily leaving behind their own. The perception of others has many benefits. First, recognizing research that illustrates a growing decline of health is a first step. Our future teachers should be keenly aware of the epidemic of chronic diseases and how they can be prevented. Knowledge of the present and future benefits of physical activity is also paramount. Increased activity leads to increased health in people of all ages (USDHHS, 2000). Empathic awareness could help preservice teachers understand the painful recollections and negative image of humiliating PE experiences in order to revise traditional programs into a more user-friendly PE where all students have the potential to succeed. Awareness of sociometric status and learned helplessness could help future teachers to be mindful of the potential social and psychological damage that can occur in PE and avoid setting up their students to fail, thus reducing the incidents of public humiliation. Empathic awareness also could allow our future teachers focus on a student-centered practice designed to accommodate a diversity of ability in their classrooms. Studies have shown student outcomes are positively correlated with teachers who are able to "read" students' understandings and adjust practice accordingly (Aspy & Roebuck, 1977; Okeefe and Johnston 1989).

In practical terms, an improvement in higher-order empathy (ECPT) represents a possible advancement toward Hoffman's (1987) fourth stage of empathy development, *empathy for another's life condition*. Whereas in stage three, *empathy for another's feelings*, empathy may be limited to those persons with similar situations to that of the empathizer (i.e., a PE teacher identifying and emphasizing with athletic students), stage four empathy expands to a broader range of targets, such as groups of people different than the empathizer (Hoffman, 2000). A PE teacher displaying higher-order empathy may be better situated to use his/her empathic capacity to increase understanding of a diversity of students' situations and increase feelings of positive regard for students' success in the PE class. This could lead to a more trusting and non-threatening learning environment which could increase participation levels. In PE, more participation equals more physical activity. Promoting and enhancing empathy in teacher education programs which, in turn, leads to increased interest and participation among PE students could set the stage for a physically fit society.

81

Setting the stage for prosocial development and action

While empathy can be regarded as recognition of others' feelings and situations, it doesn't automatically translate to helping behaviors. However, the fostering of empathic predispositions is an important step in the development of social responsibility (Berman, 1998). Citing its' highly interactive and emotional nature, many educators consider PE to be the ideal setting for the development of social qualities (Cutforth and Parker, 1996; Shapiro & Lawson, 1982; Gibbons & Bressan, 1991; Gerdes, 2001). Furthermore, Hoffman's highest stage of empathic development, "empathy for another's life condition" (as represented in the IRI composite score ECPT) is considered the developmental foundation for altruistic behavior (Hoffman, 2000; Morrell, 2003) and is considered congruent with moral action, which is personified by caring for others in a helping capacity. Caring is essential to education as it is considered a moral and cultural value that guides us in the perception and interaction of others (Noddings, 1992; Noblit et al., 1995). One of the primary aims of education is to produce good, productive citizens. Empathy leads to caring, which leads to helping, which leads to greater civic involvement, which is the basis for democratic society. In that sense, this study could also be considered an initial attempt to answer President Obama's challenge to address the "empathy deficit," which "blinds many to the plight of struggling members of society" (Pluvoise, 2006, p. 1) by finding opportunities to help the public good.

With physical education's social nature and propensity to teach the "whole child," it is a potentially ideal setting for developing and promoting moral character development in students (Solomon, 2004). PE could take the lead in addressing issues of physical, social, and emotional inequalities through empathy, leading to understanding and positive change.

Study strengths and limitations

Study strengths

The results of this study suggest improvement in quantitative and qualitative-measured levels of empathy among experimental group subjects. However, rather than proclaiming success, these results may best be viewed as a beginning of a new dialogue in education. Since this can be considered an initial attempt at studying empathy in PE, many things can certainly be improved. Nevertheless, there were also some things that stood out as strong points. The following points were strengths of this study:

1. The use of the IRI scale for quantitative purposes allowed the research to be conducted with an established valid and reliable measurement tool representing a multidemensional view of empathy. Results from the present study paralleled past empathy studies using the IRI scale in bullying prevention (Espelage et al., 2003), psychology (Davis, 1980), and counseling (Hatcher et al., 1994). Furthermore, the use of the higher-order empathy score (ECPT) allowed consideration of the interactive association of affective empathy (represented by EC) and

83

cognitive empathy (represented by PT). The importance of higher-order

empathy is expressed by Davis (1996), Hoffman (2000), Morril (2003),

and others as being congruent with caring and altruistic behavior which

is considered an essential ingredient of democratic education (Kohn,

1990; Morril, 2003; Noblit et al., Noddings, 1992).

2. Mixed methods: The use of quantitative and qualitative mixed methods

research allowed for two different approaches to be focused on the

same occurrence – the development of empathy. In addition to the

quantitative IRI scale, the study employed a qualitative reflective essay

measurement. Since empathy is considered (at least in part) an affective

construct, and written expression is considered an effective way to

measure affective outcomes (Cutforth & Parker, 1996), the

measurement of subjects' expressed feelings may more likely occur

through a written reflection. With the focus of the essay being a

description of "four words," keywords were easily ascertainable. In

addition, the subsequent posttest reflection allowed the researcher

anecdotal information detailing the perceived change (or lack thereof)

that occurred during the course of the study.

The results of each method appeared to be complementary, as the

quantitative analysis of IRI scores appeared to be consistent with

subjects' reflective essays. Specifically, the significant change in IRI

scores mirrored the most dramatic change in subject reflection among the experimental group, while little to no change in IRI scores mirrored an overall "no change" statement among control groups. Either method alone would not have exhibited the same strength of evidence as the corroboration of the mixed methods findings.

3. The study was designed to control several threats to internal validity. Primarily, a control group was used in conjunction with a comparison (experimental) group in order to help control for external threats such as researcher bias and maturation. The subjects came from three universities with similar teacher education programs. Subject groups comprised of similar average age, gender ratio, ethnicity ratio, and college year. All groups participated in a program-required elementary methods course using the same textbook, a similar course of study, and included a field-experience component. All classes were conducted on the same days during the same time period (Tuesdays & Thursdays, Spring, 2009 semester). Both experimental and control group courses were implemented in a natural context with the experimental group receiving an additional imbedded curriculum.

Secondly, a pre-test/post-test design was used with measurements taken before and after treatment. The pre-test data on empathy (both quantitative and qualitative) allowed for control of pre-existing variations between the two groups. In addition, confidentiality measures were taken to ensure that the researcher and course

85

instructors did not have access to the coded subject roster and could not link subject identities with their responses. An IRB-trained graduate assistant was employed to deploy, collect, sort, and code subject surveys and essays. Although random assignment was not used to place students into the experiment and control groups, several features support their equivalence.

4. Response rates were strong among all groups, supporting good external validity.

5. Subjects were studied at the college level, which is considered the optimal developmental period for higher-order empathy (Hatcher et al., 1994; Hoffman, 1987). This allowed the researcher the best opportunity to view a potential developmental shift between lower and higher forms of empathy. The results of the current study appear to demonstrate this shift among experimental group subjects and highlight the effect of the focused intervention in bringing about the desired change.

6. Another possible strength of this study was the augmentation of the core course curriculum in the experimental groups (consisting of in-class didactic lessons, films and activities) with in class and out-of-class field experiences working with elementary school children. All

groups were enrolled in courses that employed a field experience

component. Since empathy develops through social interaction

(Hoffman, 2000; Hunt, 2007), social engagement is considered critical

in the study of empathy development (O'Keefe & Johnston, 1989).

Practical experiences in the field allow subjects to be immersed in

another environment in order to better see and understand someone

else's point of view (McAllister & Irvine, 2002). It could also serve to

give subjects real-world examples of the principles learned in class.

Several other empathy education studies have reported success using a

classroom model augmented with social interactions (Batson et al.,

1997; Cutcliffe & Cassedy 1999; Håkansson & Montgomery, 2003;

McAllister & Irvine, 2002). This should be seen as important

considering the subject choice to be educators. Since teaching is a

human-services endeavor, pre-service teachers could be considered

better prepared to serve the needs of their future students if their

training extends beyond the sole acquisition of content knowledge

(Darling-Hammond, 2003).

Study limitations

This study had several limitations, as listed below.

1. The sample size (N = 59) was much smaller than expected, which

    potentiually limits the power of the study. This could potentially have

    led Type II errors for the non-significant inferential tests. The small

    sample may not have been associated with adequate power to show a

87

difference between experimental and control group means.
Demographic comparisons were also limited in this study. Although
evenly dispersed among groups, gender differences (male = 71%,
females = 29%) were disproportional to the larger college population,
making it difficult to study potential differences between gender.
Furthermore, ethnic homogeneity, with 88% of subjects describing
themselves as white/ Caucasian, ruled out further investigation of
differences on specific populations. Future studies with larger samples
may ensure greater power to potentially detect a greater range of
effects. Recruitment of other PETE programs for study could possibly
increase the number of subjects, improve gender ratio, and involve
more ethnically diverse subjects.

2. Subjects were not randomly assigned to experimental and control
   groups, instead intact classrooms were utilized. With use of the intact
   classrooms, direct control of the actual instruction was not available. In
   addition, three different faculty members instructed the four groups,
   one each for the experimental groups and one for the two control
   groups. Although the control groups were instructed by the same
   person and used the same text book, outside of the course syllabi, this
   study did not address specific differences between the two control
   groups. The convenient sampling of intact groups and associated lack
   of randomization is a limitation of the study design. Improvement in

this regard would focus on greater use of covariates to statistically equate the control and experimental groups on potentially confounding variables.

3. The study took place during a single semester and did not have a long-term follow-up component. Since empathy is developmental, it may be more advantageous to conduct a longer term study. Ideally, a study of this nature could begin in freshman year (introduction to PE course) and run through senior year (student teaching). This approach would allow for differentiation between the effects of an empathy intervention verses the natural development of empathy through maturity. Another important consideration would be following pre-service teachers' development and application of empathy into their first three years of teaching. Since the ultimate goal of empathy development in pre-service PE teachers is to improve the physical fitness of their future students and eventually the fitness of those students as adults, longitudinal research designs are indicated. Further discussion of this longitudinal research considerations appear in #5 below.

4. The content of the experimental group intervention was delivered by two different instructors, including the researcher. Since there was no mechanism in place to verify that the curriculum was the same, differentiated instruction of the same material may have led to

differences in subject replies. A possible example of this occurred with the covering of the "Carl Rogers: Student-centered education" lesson. While the instructor of experimental group 1 elaborated on the specific teaching points of the lesson, experimental group 2 instructor characterized his treatment of this content to "strictly sticking to the points presented on the paper." It is not known how important this particular content was but it was the only lesson in the intervention curriculum that mentioned the concept of empathy. No other film, article, or hand-out spelled out "empathy." Another identified difference between the two intervention groups, was a weekly reflection assignment for the Experimental group 1. In analysis, this study did not address differences between the two experimental groups. It will be important in the future to identify key curricular components that are most effective in improving empathy with this population. Said another way, is it a specific "empathy curriculum" that is most effective, or are a variety of approaches equally useful?

Future empathy research in PETE programs may produce stronger results with a more comprehensive and standardized curriculum. Suggestions for improving the curriculum include: 1) incorporation of a specific working definition of empathy that is introduced and reinforced throughout the term of the experiment, 2) use of empathy references with explanation of how this concept relates to the PE situation throughout the curriculum, 3) outside speakers to voice personal perceptions (positive and negative) of PE experiences to the subjects, and 4) written subject reflection on topics covered in lessons. Decreasing the variability among experimental group instructors in delivery of a more comprehensive curriculum will also strengthen future research. Training of experimental group instructors including review and discussion of key curriculum components is recommended.

5. The ultimate outcome of interest is the improvement of students in PE classes (physical fitness, activity levels, inclination stay physically active) and lifelong fitness levels; this study did not look at any long term outcomes of students taught by the study subjects. As previously stated, longitudinal research is needed to determine if an empathetic PE teacher helps develop more active and physically fit students and if that carries over to adult life. To address the first part of the longitudinal question, college freshmen entering a PETE program as could be given the pre-test IRI survey (pre-test), then participate in a four-year teacher-preparation program with embedded empathy curriculum, and be given the IRI survey at the completion of student teaching or beyond (post-test). In turn, once they are teaching, their students could be surveyed to determine their present interest in physical activity and their inclination to exercise in the future. Such a study could involve K-12 PE programs taught by empathy-educated teachers in comparison to K-12 PE

programs taught by teachers without an empathy aspect in their pre-service education.

Suggestions for further research and practice

Although significant results were found in this study, suggested improvements for future research are listed below

1. The current study incorporated a curriculum into an existing PE methods course. Since participation in the study was voluntary, it is likely that subjects were preoccupied with the demands and responsibilities of the actual course content. A methods course is usually comprised of methods and procedures considered essential for work as a teacher. Students enrolled in educational methods courses are usually preparing to student teach soon after, therefore acquisition of the required materials and methods is often considered paramount to other "non essential" subject matter. It is recommended that developing empathy may be more comprehensive if presented as the focal point of an entire course, as was the case with Hatcher's (1994) study.

2. Further studies could also be improved with larger numbers of subjects, greater diversity of ethnicity, and equal representation of gender. Greater numbers would increase statistical power of future studies and could allow researchers the luxury of randomly assigning

participants. More social variance could lead to further investigation of empathy and specific ethnic, cultural, or socioeconomic backgrounds. Increased gender participation could continue investigation of empathy and gender differences.

3. Tighten the empathy curriculum: As previously mentioned, the curriculum of the present study could have been more comprehensive. Subjects should be provided with a working definition of "empathy" and be given the opportunity to expand upon the concept through class discussion. In addition, instructors of curriculum content should be better coordinated with regards to delivering information. Instructors of the content will probably be best served if they are able to practice, as well as teach the concept of empathy.

4. It should also be noted that PE is likely not the only academic subject in need of empathy. Research of empathy and other subjects, either within a discipline, comparison, or cross-disciplinary, could also lead to insight on the present role of empathy (or lack thereof) in education.

In summary, as PE teacher education programs continue to seek and implement ways to improve, this study offers optimism and encouragement for the teachability and practice of empathy in a PE setting. Although historically

93

teacher education programs do not focus on affective development, results of this study could be viewed as evidence supporting its inclusion. Specifically, if higher developmental empathy leads to increased moral development and altruistic behaviors, then at the very least, more studies of this nature should be encouraged in teacher education. Overall, results of this study found significant intervention effects on quantitative and qualitative measures of empathy development. However, this should be considered just a beginning. Additional research is needed to further explore these results and expand upon the exploration of empathy development as a means to improve teacher education.

Consent Approval Form

Doctoral Dissertation Project

Dear Student,

My name is Tony Monahan and I am a graduate student at the University of Rhode Island. You are being invited to take part in a research study based on teacher education in physical education.

If you agree to be in this study, at the beginning of the semester you will be asked to answer a 28-item survey inquiring about your thoughts and feelings in a variety of situations. You may skip any question. You will also be asked to write an essay about your thoughts and feelings about your future classroom. At the end of the semester, you will again be again asked to answer a 28-item survey and write an essay.

There are very few, if any, risks involved with this study. Even though there may be no direct benefit to you for taking part in this study, the results may shed positive light on improvement in the teaching profession.

Your part in this study is anonymous meaning no one else will know if you were in this study and no one else can find out what answers you gave. A representative will be administering and collecting the surveys and essays. I will have no knowledge of your answers. Your name will never appear anywhere in any research studies that may be published. All the records for this study will be stored safely and locked in my office for a minimum of three years.

If you do decide to participate, you can always drop out of the study at any time. Whatever you decide will not be held against you in any way. No one will be upset if you don't want to participate or even if you change your mind later and want to step. If you want to quit the study, just let your professor know.

Signing your name at the bottom of this form means that you have read or listened to what it says and you understand it. Signing this form also means that you agree to participate in this study and your questions have been answered. You will be given a copy of this form after you have signed it. If you have further questions, you may contact me at 401-874-5450 or you may also contact the URI Vice President for Research at 401-874-4238.

_____   _____
Signature of Participant   Signature of Researcher

_____   _____
Typed/Printed Name   Typed/Printed Name

_____   _____
Date   Date

Student Survey

Spring Semester, 2009

Preliminary Information

1. Gender: M ( ) F ( )

2. Age: ____

3. Ethnicity: _____

4. College Year: 1 ( ) 2 ( ) 3 ( ) 4 ( ) 5 ( )

5. Is this course required or optional? Required ( ) Optional ( )

6. Do you consider yourself to be an athletic person? Yes ( ) No ( )

INTERPERSONAL REACTIVITY INDEX

The following statements inquire about your thoughts and feelings in a variety of situations. For each item, indicate how well it describes you by choosing the appropriate letter on the scale at the top of the page: A, B, C, D, or E. When you have decided on your answer, fill in the letter on the answer sheet next to the item number. READ EACH ITEM CAREFULLY BEFORE RESPONDING. Answer as honestly as you can. Thank you.

A	B	C	D	E
DOES NOT DESCRIBE ME WELL				DESCRIBES ME VERY WELL

1. I daydream and fantasize, with some regularity, about things that might happen to me.

A	B	C	D	E

2. I often have tender, concerned feelings for people less fortunate than me.

A	B	C	D	E

3. I sometimes find it difficult to see things from the "other guy's" point of view.

A	B	C	D	E

4. Sometimes I don't feel very sorry for other people when they are having problems.

A	B	C	D	E

5. I really get involved with the feelings of the characters in a novel

                      A   B   C   D   E

6. In emergency situations, I feel apprehensive and ill-at-ease.

                      A   B   C   D   E

7. I am usually objective when I watch a movie or play, and I don't often get completely caught up in it.

                      A   B   C   D   E

8. I try to look at everybody's side of a disagreement before I make a decision.

                      A   B   C   D   E

9. When I see someone being taken advantage of, I feel kind of protective towards them.

                      A   B   C   D   E

10. I sometimes feel helpless when I am in the middle of a very emotional situation.

        A   **B**   **C**   **D**   **E**

11. I sometimes try to understand my friends better by imagining how things look from their perspective.

        A   **B**   **C**   **D**   **E**

12. Becoming extremely involved in a good book or movie is somewhat rare for me.

        A   **B**   **C**   **D**   **E**

13. When I see someone get hurt, I tend to remain calm.

        A   **B**   **C**   **D**   **E**

14. Other people's misfortunes do not usually disturb me a great deal.

A   B   C   D   E

15. If I'm sure I'm right about something, I don't waste much time listening to other people's arguments.

A   B   C   D   E

16. After seeing a play or movie, I have felt as though I were one of the characters.

A   B   C   D   E

17. Being in a tense emotional situation scares me.

A   B   C   D   E

18. When I see someone being treated unfairly, I sometimes don't feel very much pity for them.

A   B   C   D   E

19. I am usually pretty effective in dealing with emergencies

A   B   C   D   E

20. I am often quite touched by things that I see happen.

A   B   C   D   E

21. I believe that there are two sides to every question and try to look at them both.

A   B   C   D   E

22. I would describe myself as a pretty soft-hearted person.

       A   B   C   D   E

23. When I watch a good movie, I can very easily put myself in the place of a leading character.

       A   B   C   D   E

24. I tend to lose control during emergencies.

       A   B   C   D   E

25. When I am reading an interesting story or novel, I imagine how I would feel if the events in the story were happening to me.

       A   B   C   D   E

26. When I see someone who badly needs help in an emergency, I go to pieces.

A   B   C   D   E

27. Before criticizing somebody, I try to imagine how I would feel if I were in their place.

A   B   C   D   E

THANK YOU!

Student Essay
Spring Semester, 2009

Choose four descriptive words you hope your students would use to describe you as a teacher.

1.

2.

3.

4.

APPENDIX D

Read your essay from the beginning of the semester and compare it to the one you just wrote. Reflect upon similarities or differences between the two. What things changed? What things stayed the same?

APPENDIX E

Student Essay: Choose four descriptive words you hope your students would use to describe you as a teacher.

Essay reflection (post essay only): **Read your essay from the beginning of the semester and compare it to the one you just wrote. Reflect upon similarities or differences between the two. What things changed? What things stayed the same?**

CONTROL GROUPS

Subject	Essay 1: January, 2009	Essay 2: May, 2009	Reflection: May 2009
HU1-01	1. Interesting – I would hope my students think I am an interesting teacher and like to participate in my class. 2. Fun – When I'm a teacher I wouldn't want my students dreading my class, but instead look forward to coming. 3. Interactive – I would like to help my students learn about PE and show them anything they might be unable to do. 4. Knowledgeable – When I'm a teacher I would to know a lot about the subject matter and be able to answer all	1. Fun – When I'm a teacher I hope the students find me fun. 2. Interesting – I hope my students think I'm interesting and are eager to come to my class. 3. Helping – I hope to help any of my students that need it. 4. Knowledgeable – I hope to have my students feel that I know a great deal about the subject matter.	Pretty much everything stayed the same in my hopes for my students.

	questions my students have.		
HU1-02	1. Fun – I want my students to know I'm fun and will never bore them. 2. Funny – I want my students to know I'm funny and can make jokes with them. 3. Energized – I hope students see me as energized in every activity. 4. Focused – I hope students see I am focused on changing their health and lifestyle.	1. Energetic 2. Respectful 3. Fun 4. Passionate	Everything stayed the same except "passionate." I think passion is important in teaching.
HU1-03	1. Fit – in shape, healthy, etc. 2. Smart – knows a lot about fitness, sports, etc. 3. Athletic – is good at demonstrations. 4. Fair – always grades fair, does not favor athletes and gives everyone a chance to succeed.	1. Athletic 2. Awesome 3. Fun 4. Fair	No change
HU1-04	1. Energetic – I would bring tons of energy to my classes to keep the attention of students. 2. Interesting – I	1. Interesting 2. Spontaneous 3. Exciting 4. Creative	Everything stayed the same. I think the qualities I would like to be described as are essential for educators to have. Having the

	would relate skills and lessons to everyday situations that they could use. 3. Spontaneous – having the ability to change the direction of class to better improve it. 4. Creative – finding unique and interesting ways to convey the message/ key point of lessons.		characteristics would help develop a greater relationship with students.
HU1-05	1. Leader – I hope my students look up to me as a positive influence and role model. 2. Knowledgeable – I hope my students can easily observe the wide range of my content knowledge while I'm teaching. 3. Creative – I want to provide creative, interesting, and exciting activities to help motivate my students to live a healthy active lifestyle for the rest of their lives. 4. Responsible – I want my students to have the	1. Creative 2. Intelligent 3. Role Model 4. Responsible	I still wrote "responsible" and "creative," which stayed the same since last time. I also wrote "knowledgeable" and "leader," this time "intelligent" and "role model." They have the same meaning. I still feel the same way.

	perspective that I am a responsible adult and role model rather than a friend. Too many young teachers fail to draw the appropriate boundary lines.		
HU1-06	1. Motivational – I would like to be able to encourage my students to get involved in class and outside of class. 2. Fun – I want my students to enjoy themselves while learning in class. 3. Fair – I think all students must be treated equally. Playing favorites harms the learning experience. 4. Effective – if my lessons and teaching styles aren't effective then my job as a PE teacher has not been fulfilled.	Not present for post essay	Not present for post essay
HU1-07	1. Caring – I try to meet everyone's needs and to make sure they are comfortable in their/ my class. 2. Enthusiastic – I	1. Enthusiastic – I want them to see I enjoy what I'm doing. 2. Kind – I treat everyone with the respect they deserve.	Everything stayed the same except for "knowledge." That was the word that was different.

110

	have a love of sports and fitness and I use the enthusiasm I have to help kids excel and get better for themselves. 3. Loyal – I am always a person that students can come to for anything they need. 4. Knowledgeable – Students will realize that I have a great knowledge of sports and fitness activities to help them succeed.	3. Honest – people, especially students can put their trust in me. 4. Loyal – I will help out any students who need it.	
HU1-10	1. Responsible – I a very responsible person and I want my students to know I as a PE teacher will provide quality teaching for all my students. 2. Caring – I care about my students and if they are ever in needs, I will try to help them in all my power. 3. 4.	1. Respectful, protective, emotional, and understanding. 2. 3. 4.	Everything changed.
HU1-11	1. Motivational – in the sense that I'd be the kind of teacher that	Not present for post essay	Not present for post essay

	encourages and students to fully participate in a positive and fun manner. When being motivational it is important that it is in a positive manner. 2. Being <u>caring</u> is important in the sense that not only is it the right thing to do, it will typically make students comfortable and more at ease. 3. It is important that your students see you as <u>fun</u>. Students are more apt to want to learn in an environment where the material instructor are both fun. 4. The most important aspect students should recognize is a teacher that is <u>knowledgeable</u> about the material. Students will be way more receptive to a confident teacher that knows his/her material.		
HU1-12	1. Understanding –	1. Exciting – I	Nothing has

	I would hope my students know that I understand society and what troubles they might be going through at a particular time. 2. Helpful – I am there to help the students succeed at any task they have. Helping students reach their goals is a big part of a teacher. 3. Professional – I would hope they look at me as a professional figure who presents himself very well. 4. Fun – I am fun and know how to get children involved in every activity.	always want to be exciting and come up with new ideas. 2. Enthusiastic – by being enthusiastic children keep interested in the activity. 3. Understanding – understand the children and what is going on. 4. Caring – always have an open door for children to talk to.	changed. My feelings have stayed the same.
HU1-13	1. Leader – in the sense that I do things in my own way. I set a good example and have others want to follow my example. 2. Compassionate – that I love my work and take it seriously. I would hope they see I care about the matter at hand.	1. Prepared 2. Consistent 3. Respectable 4. Honest	No change

	3. Effective – I am fully prepared and I get my point across clearly with composure. 4. Knowledgeable – I know the subject at hand in every aspect. I can answer questions effectively and clearly.		
HU1-14	1. Helpful – always being there when they have a problem whether it be school or non-school related. 2. Inspiring – have a positive influence on their life. When they think of phys ed to think of me and the role I played in their life-long decisions. 3. Fun – kids want to come to my class and look forward to it. Have everyone involved and having a good time. 4. Effective – I taught them what they needed/wanted to learn in a way that they will	1. Fun to be around 2. Excited to go to class. 3. Leave an impact on their lives. 4. Be a role model.	Mostly the same. I want to be a fun teacher. I want to be inspiring or a role model. I want to be effective and leave an impact on their lives, and I want to be helpful.

	never forget.		
HU1-15	1. Motivating – I want to be able to motivate the students to participate without pressuring them. 2. Caring – I'm concerned about the students inside the classroom as well as outside. 3. Fun – make activities fun so students can enjoy themselves. 4. Knowledgeable – want students to feel they are actually learning something important.	1. Creative – I hope my students feel that I bring out the best imagination. 2. Enthusiastic about teaching. 3. Effective – gets students to participate. 4. Caring – care about the students.	It seems most of the descriptions are similar.
HU1-16	1. Caring – want my students to know I want them to succeed and will take the time to help improve or give help for phys ed related problems outside phys ed. 2. Energetic – want students to see and feel off my energy. See that physical education is fun in all areas and just cause your not a star athlete	1. Same 2. 3. 4.	I did not change my characteristic. My intentions/ purpose for teaching are and will always remain the same. Want to bring energy, warm environment, trust, and professionalism to my classroom.

	doesn't mean phys ed can't be enjoyable. 3. Knowledgeable – students trust that I know the content I am teaching. 4. Professional – want students to understand that I am a teacher and must treat me with same respect and authority I treat them with and that they treat other teachers with. Also to see me as a role model and feed off all my energy, care and knowledge not only in PE but in life.		
HU1-17	1. I would hope that my students would think of me as a personable teacher. I want them to be able to come to me not just to talk about physical education but other things or situations they may be dealing with in their life. 2. I hope my students see me as a role-model. I	1. Fun – I want students to <u>want</u> to come to my class and enjoy it. 2. Personable – if a student has a problem I want to be there for them if they need help. 3. Creative – as a teacher I should do creative activities. 4. Leader (role-model) – I want students to look up to me.	Basically everything stayed the same.

	want to be a leader and good example for my students because I know my physical education teachers were to me, which encouraged me to enter this field. 3. I hope I am fun. I want students to want to come to my class and enjoy the activities that I have planned. 4. I want my students to think I am creative. Class is a lot more enjoyable if the activities are new, interesting, and exciting to your students.		
HU2-01	1. I would want my students to say I was fun and that the class was fun. 2. I hope they find my class interesting. 3. I hope they find me and my class informing and helpful. 4. I would hope they say I am very knowledgeable about the subject.	1. Fun 2. Interesting 3. Helpful 4. Knowledgeable	It is pretty much the same. I still want my students to think I am fun, knowledgeable, helpful, and think my class is interested.
HU2-02	1. Fun	1. Knowledgeable	Relatively no

117

	2. Cool 3. Intelligent 4. Organized	2. Fun 3. Intelligent 4. Funny	change.
HU2-03	1. Caring 2. Understanding 3. Helpful 4. Encouraging	1. Caring 2. Helpful 3. Encouraging 4. Motivating	I would continue to be helpful and as encouraging as possible. I feel this is vital to one's future. If you are "brought down" at a young age, that will carry with you throughout your life.
HU2-04	1. Creative – always have something on my mind. Give the students something new to experience. 2. Knowledgeable – I know my field pretty well when it comes to things I'm interested in I will succeed. 3. Leader – I will always strive to go the furthest, never give up. 4. Enthusiastic – I will help the kids adapt to the concept, give them different test and make it fun.	1. Enthusiastic 2. Caring 3. Motivated 4. Creative	No change.
HU2-05	1. 2. 3. 4.	1. Real 2. Dude 3. Stud 4. Weird	I just feel way more real and studly.

118

HU2-06	1. Exciting 2. Fun 3. 4.	1. Funny 2. Smart 3. Exciting 4. Respectable	There was no change.
HU2-07	1. Fun 2. Caring 3. Interesting 4. The reason why they want to come to class.	1. Fun 2. Smart 3. Organized 4. Nice	No change
HU2-08	1. Caring – I chose this word because I hope students would they could come to me with any issue. Students that have teachers that "don't" care cause their relationship to be strained, not open and cold. 2. Knowledgeable – I hope my students would think that I am knowledgeable about the subject I am teaching. 3. Professional – I hope my students feel that I have a good classroom environment that is fun but yet when things have to get done they will because the students respect me as a professional. 4. Athletic – being	Not present for post essay	Not present for post essay

	that I want to become a physical education teacher I hope my students feel that I am somewhat athletic.		
HU2-12	1. Creative – I hope that my students would describe me as a creative teacher who is able to cater to the needs of each student incorporating new ideas and concepts into each lesson. 2. Motivational – I hope that students would describe me as motivational, as through my teachings they would be motivated to compete in physical activity and learn more about the area. 3. Friendly – I hope that my students would describe me friendly and above feel free to talk to me about anything they need to talk to me about. 4. Inspirational – I hope that my students would	1. Caring 2. Energetic 3. Passionate 4. Understanding	Both essays have similarities in terms of the words used. I the first essay I wrote "creative," "motivational," "friendly." And "inspirational." In the second essay I wrote "caring," "energetic," "passionate," and "understanding." The first sets of answers were more personal and were views that I wanted students to have of me. In contrast, the second sets of answers were more extensive, and how I wanted to feel towards others. I wanted to be more caring and understanding.

120

	find me inspirational and use me as a role model, someone to look up to and realize the options open for female athletes.		
HU2-13	1. Fun 2. Creative 3. Enjoyable 4. Friendly	1. Fun/enjoyable 2. Inspiring 3. Funny 4. Playful	My thought process has not changed about how I want my students to view me.
HU2-14	1. Fun – I hope my students enjoy my class and enjoy coming to it each day. 2. Meaningful – I hope my student take something out of my class. 3. Interesting – I hope my students can find new things they like that I teach 4.	1. Fun 2. Creative 3. Awesome 4. Interesting	No change

EXPERIMENTAL GROUPS

Subject	Essay 1: January, 2009	Essay 2: May, 2009	Reflection: May 2009
URI-01	1. Trustworthy 2. Helpful 3. Reliable 4. Passionate	1. Empathy 2. Emotional 3. Knowledge 4. Thoughtful	Empathy was the main difference I noticed. Putting yourself in the students' perspective is the key. Being an affective teacher was the main difference. However, what I noticed is empathy is the most important

121

				aspect of being a great teacher.
URI-02	1. Trustworthy 2. Funny 3. Dedicated 4. Enthusiastic 5. Knowledgeable	1. Inspirational 2. Role model/ dependable 3. Hard Working 4. Funny 5. Passionate		All of the words I used to describe how I want to be valued as a teacher are similar. The first time I had more specific words where this time around it's a number of traits that make a good role model, inspirational person, etc. I hope my students one day value me in these ways some day.
URI-03	1. Fun 2. Caring 3. Encouraging 4. Motivated	1. Empathetic 2. Encouraging 3. Enthusiastic 4. Caring		I noticed I changed 2 of my words from fun and motivating to empathetic and enthusiastic. I feel as a person I want to make a difference in others and that was my main goal. It is important to be a good role model for others and I want to encourage others to do the best they can.
URI-04	1. Fun 2. Energetic 3. Trusting 4. Imaginative	1. Fun for all 2. Energetic- to show I'm interested in the students' 3. Passionate about my class 4. Enthusiastic about subjects taught		I still have the words energetic and fun. The difference in the beginning was trusting and imaginative and now passionate and enthusiastic.
URI-05	1. Fun 2. Energetic	1. Energetic 2. Passionate – If I		I am more concerned with empathy and

122

	3. Caring 4. Respectful	am excited about what I am doing they will be too. 3. Empathetic – understand what students are going through 4. Kind	understanding different students' situations rather than just being fun and exciting. I am more concerned with my quality of teaching rather than how students perceive me.
URI-06	1. Trustworthy 2. Funny 3. Calm 4. Respectful	1. Approachable 2. Honest 3. Insightful 4. Fun	I replaced trustworthy with honest. I think the two are somewhat interchangeable. I had funny on the first one and replaced it with fun because I would rather my students have a good time than having them think I'm funny. I added insightful this time because I want to be able to answer my students' questions. Going along with that I want my students to feel comfortable approaching me with questions or problems.
URI-07	1. Fun 2. Understanding 3. Fair 4. Motivating	Not present for post essay	Not present for post essay
URI-08	1. Respectful 2. Fun 3. Motivating 4. Good listener	1. Respect – respect is key and should be displayed for students and teachers. 2. Empathy – as a teacher you must	Similar but now it's much more deep and in depth. At first I wrote those 4 words because I thought they were things that were important. Now I know they are

123

		be able to put yourself in your students' shoes. 3. Knowledge – must have a firm background in content area. 4. Hot dog! A general positive feeling at the end of a productive class.	important and necessary for a productive class.
URI-09	1. Fun 2. Interesting 3. Motivational 4. Easy to talk to	1. Fun 2. Empathetic 3. Respectful 4. Motivational	I had a couple of similarities and a couple of differences. I have become more understanding of individual differences and more empathetic for each individual.
URI-10	1. Caring 2. Helpful 3. Outgoing 4. Fun	1. Energetic 2. Fun 3. Informative 4. Motivating	Things that changed was I added energetic because the students feed off your energy and if you are upbeat they will be too. You have to motivate your students to do well. If not they will not try hard and try new things. I still said fun because I want all my students to have fun and learn.
URI-11	1. Fun – I want to be able to teach effectively with being fun and not just hard-nosed about it. 2. Creative – One thing that I am not right now	1. Stupendous 2. Caring 3. Fun 4. Amazing	My words the second time was more praising rather than words that would describe what a good teacher does. The only one that was the same was "fun."

124

	but would like to learn. 3. Organized – not being puzzled while teaching. 4. Confident – I don't want to seem scared to teach.		
URI-14	1. Knowledgeable 2. Empathetic 3. Fair 4. Fun	1. Effective – I hope to be able to use relevant ideas and concepts to teach <u>all</u> of my students. 2. Empathetic – I want my students to know I will try to understand how they feel and if they have a question or problem they could talk to me about it. 3. Knowledgeable – I want to have a variety of "tools" to teach my students. I want to have plan B, C, D, etc., just in case. 4. Fair – I want my students to feel safe in my class to experiment and learn about their environment – without feeling penalized for "not doing it	Surprisingly most of the words I chose were the same and in the same order. I dropped fun from the second one. I know my class will be fun. I don't have to put so much pressure on the fun factor, it will just happen. That's the beauty of PE! I traded that for effective. I know how to plan age, developmentally appropriate activities. I also know that it is very important to plan and assess and those are the tools to being effective.

		right."	
URI-15	1. Empathetic 2. Dependable 3. Effective 4. Caring	1. Empathetic 2. Fun 3. Fair 4. Awesome 5. Caring	There were two same responses from my first to second reflections. Caring and empathetic have always been my focus as a teacher. A shift has been in my desire to be more fun and exciting compared to just good in content.
URI-16	1. Caring 2. Fun 3. Creative 4. Greatest	1. Caring 2. Best 3. Fun 4. Fair	Most were the same but one changed from creative to fair.
URI-17	1. Caring 2. Helpful 3. Fun 4. Creative	1. Compassionate 2. Fun 3. Knowledgeable 4. Fair	The most important aspects did not have a big change. Compassion and fun are still my most important parts of being a good PE teacher. The things on each are both very important in my eyes, but I feel on a daily basis those words might slightly differ.
URI-18	1. Confident 2. Intelligent 3. Energetic 4. Amusing	1. Empathetic – I want students to feel like I care about their well-being. 2. Fun – want students to enjoy my class. 3. Understanding – I want students to feel comfortable	All of my answers were different. My new answers are a reflection to more caring about what the student thinks rather than myself.

		when coming to me. 4. Enthusiastic-don't want to be boring.	
URI-20	1. Approachable 2. Friendly 3. Caring 4. Fun	1. Caring 2. Fun 3. Empathetic 4. Organized	After reflecting on my previous essay, I have the same characteristics of caring, fun and approachable. I feel that these are qualities that I take pride in and that help me as a teacher. New qualities that I have learned to better help me as a teacher are organization and knowledge of understanding my students. Being empathetic toward my students will help me understand them and help me as a teacher get them to be the best they can be.
URI-21	1. Effective 2. Professional 3. Trustworthy 4. Responsible	1. Empathetic 2. Caring 3. Honest 4. Fair	All of these words are similar. In the end, the words are how every student would want a teacher to be. I learned empathy in this class and brought that into my characteristics because I want to put myself in their shoes. This also comes down to fairness, which is why I brought that in.

ECSU-01	1. Effective – I want students to believe my teaching methods are effective. 2. Influential – I hope to have a major influence on the students 3. Respectful – I want students to feel like I respect them as individuals 4. Fun – I want students to enjoy being around me and what I teach them.	1. Dedicated – someone that is dedicated to bringing out the best in the students at all times. 2. Leader – Someone who demonstrates leadership qualities. 3. Effective – someone whose lessons and teachings are effective for an individual and group. 4. Helpful – Someone that students find helpful in all situations.	I found both of these essays quite similar even though there are some differences in word selection. One descriptive word I used in both was "effective." In the first one I put "influential" and the second I had put "leader," which I find these two basically the same concept because when I am teaching I know there will be more than 4 descriptive words for me. Hopefully they are all positive!
ECSU-02	1. Fun - I want my students to view me as fun to be around. 2. Understanding – I want my students to come to me if they need to talk to someone. 3. Interesting - I want my students to be intrigued by me. 4. "A Good PE Teacher" – I want my students to talk about me when they are older.	1. Caring – I would like my students to think of me as a caring person. If one has a problem, or wants to talk with someone, I want one to come to me. 2. Interesting – I would like my students to think of me as interesting and funny. I want my class environment to be interesting so that class is interesting. 3. Intelligent – I	My essay from the beginning of the semester was a bit more succinct, but it touched upon many of the same points I wrote about in my second essay. In both essays I wanted my students to think of me as fun/interesting, caring, and understanding. In both essays, more so the second one, I want students to develop a relationship with me. That is the teacher I want to be. I have a lot of goals and aspirations as a

		want to be considered a "smart" person in my school. Students will come to me for advice and trust my opinion. 4. Understanding – As I mentioned in section one, I want my students to trust me, be able to talk with me, and form a relationship with me. This goes along with respect for me.	teacher and they are reflected in these essays. Thank you.
ECSU-03	1. Caring 2. Open minded 3. Role model 4. Pusher	1. Caring for students 2. Helpful towards their understanding 3. Open-mindedness for situations that might occur. 4. Understanding of their problems.	I don't think I have changed much. The words might have, but I have not. I will always be the same person and the words that describe how I feel about myself are, in my opinion, what makes a great teacher. If I were to change these thoughts about myself then I would feel that I would not be a good teacher.
ECSU-04	1. Fun 2. Intelligent 3. Caring 4. Respectful	1. Respectful – I will respect my students so they respect me. 2. Intelligent – know the material. 3. Exciting –	Some things that were similar were "respectful" and "intelligent." I think "respectful" is probably the most important and that is why I put it both

		enthusiastic about class. 4. Not boring – students look forward to coming to my class.	times. Some that changed were "fun." I put "exciting" instead which kind of means the same. I also put caring the first time but the second time I put not boring because if you are boring students won't pay attention. I think all 6 words pretty much describe me.
ECSU-05	1. Helpful- I will go out of my way to address individual needs of my students. 2. Enthusiastic – I encourage my students with a positive attitude and am always ready to teach. 3. Knowledgeable – I understand all aspects of my profession and more often than not have answers for my students. 4. Caring – I will help my students in the classroom and out.	1. Hard working – I am available to my students before and after school. I am constantly tweaking lessons to meet students' needs. 2. Intelligent – I understand my subject well and that translates well into my teaching. I am able to help students with other courses. 3. Mentor – I help students feel comfortable and am available to them to discuss concerns that happen outside the classroom. 4. Fair – I expect a lot from my students, but I am reasonable and easy to	In both I am concerned for my students in and out of the classroom. I want to feel comfortable and know that I understand my content. The second time I was concerned with my work ethic, how it affects my students. First time I was concerned how I came across to students, second time I am more concerned with how and what they learn, being a role model.

		approach with questions or concerns. Students always know where they stand with me.	
ECSU-06	1. Professional – I always carry myself as though I am in charge of people at all times. 2. Caring – I will do what I can to help others who need it. 3. Understanding – I understand different sides of situations 4. Approachable – people can come to me with any problems for help or advice or just both.	1. Fun – my classes are always the best part of their day. 2. Caring – I can help them with any problems they have. 3. Organized – My classes always run smoothly. 4. Approachable – students feel comfortable coming to me and asking for help or anything.	Being caring and approachable both stayed the same. I feel that those are very important qualities in a teacher. Instead of professional and understanding I put fun and organized because I've learned that those two are very important parts of teaching.
ECSU-07	1. Energetic – I want the students to be amazed how energized I am to work with them and that I put 100% in every activity I show them and participate in. 2. Fun – I want them to love coming to class and excited when they see me in the halls. I want them to	1. Enthusiastic – want them to see me get involved in the lesson and show through my enthusiasm that I know the material and I'm having fun. 2. Good – want them to understand that I can talk the talk and walk the walk. I know the course and am masterful at it. Overall I want to	The things that stayed the same was energy/enthusiastic and kind/respectful. I want to be respectful and energetic in my area. What changed was I went from fun and athletic to good and smart because being masterful is the key to being a great teacher. I want to be smart in other areas as well.

131

	enjoy being around me and in the room that I teach in. 3. Kind – want to see how nice and caring I am for their safety and feelings. They'll know that if they have a problem, they can tell me and if they have a question, to ask me. 4. Athletic – demonstrate to them that I can perform any activity that I teach and they expect me to complete every activity as well.	be described as a very good teacher. 3. Smart – that I know my info in my particular curriculum, such as PE, but in other areas as well; math, English, health, etc. 4. Respectful – know that they have my respect and can be open with me if there are problems.	
ECSU-08	1. Responsible 2. Reliable 3. Knowledgeable 4. Creative	1. Helpful 2. Compassionate 3. Caring 4. Intelligent	The main difference between the beginning and end of the semester was that at the beginning of the semester my descriptive words were based on what I thought a book would want a teacher to be. After this semester, not just this class, I feel like I have grown up as a person and as a teacher and found what "I" wanted to be rather than what a book tells me to be.
ECSU-09	1. Reliable – I would like my	1. Enthusiastic – because I would	Between the essays from the beginning of

132

	students to know that I will not give up on them no matter what. 2. Understanding – I want my students to know that I am not there to be the bad guy, that I am there to help better themselves. 3. Trustworthy – I want my students to know they can come to me with any situation in or out of class. 4. Fun – I want to make learning worthwhile for my students and make a lasting impression on their lives.	want my students to look forward to coming to class and wanting to learn. 2. Understanding – because I would want my students to know I am not a robot and I do care about my students. 3. Reliable – because I want my students to be able to trust me and come to me with anything they can't handle. 4. Determined – because I want my students to know that I am there to teach them certain material and for them to understand the material.	the semester to the essay now, I wrote down two words the same each time. "Reliable" and "understanding" are important features, in my opinion, for a teacher to have. Trustworthy and fun were from the beginning of the semester and were replaced by "enthusiastic" and "determined." All four of these features are considerable to what a teacher should possess.
ECSU-10	1. Role model- someone my students can look up to. 2. Fun – students enjoy coming to class and learning. 3. Friendly – a person that students feel they can talk to.	1. Role model – someone my students can look up to. 2. Fun – makes every activity fun. 3. Nice – someone my students feel they can come to at all times.	Almost both of these essays are the same. On both essays I have "leader," "fun," and "role model." The only difference is on the first essay I put "friendly and the second essay I the second essay I put "nice."

ECSU-11	1. Caring – I hope the students would think that I care about them and have their best interests in mind. 2. Fun – I would hope that my students like to come to my class and think learning with me is fun. 3. Respectful – I want my kids to know that I respect them and their feelings. 4. Knowledgeable – I want my students to know that I understand what I teach and give them a solid education.	1. Motivating – I hope I motivate the students to learn in and out of the classroom. 2. Caring – I hope the kids know I care about their feelings. 3. Nice – I hope they think I am a nice person and treat them fairly. 4. Smart – I hope they think I am knowledgeable about PE.	The only thing that changed was motivating the kids to learn even though I still think that is important. I still want the children to look and think of me as kind, respectful, and knowledgeable.
ECSU-12	1. Professional – I want them to see that I care about my job and present myself as a professional. I want them to also see the respect I have for myself. 2. Positive – I feel a positive attitude is key in the teaching profession. I want to encourage them	1. Motivated – to love what I do and continue to work hard and improve each day. 2. Adaptive – to adjust to all different needs of students. 3. Caring – to care about the needs and emotions of my students. 4. Positive – always carrying a positive attitude.	The only word that matched was "positive." I'm not surprised because I think it's the most important. If a teacher doesn't have a positive attitude than they are in the wrong profession. One word I added that I left behind that I wish I included was professional.

	as best as I can. 3. Athletic – in PE I need to be able to perform what I teach. 4. Helpful – I want to be available and as helping as I can.		
ECSU-14	1. Knowledgeable – I want my students to appreciate how much I know and am able to teach them in our field of study. 2. Caring – I want my students to know that I care about their future. 3. Approachable – I want my students to feel comfortable talking to me if they are ever in need of something. 4. Fun – I want my students to like me and get excited to have fun in my class.	1. Approachable – I hope they feel comfortable coming to talk to me. 2. Intelligent – I want my students to think I am smart and know what I am talking about. 3. Fun – I want my students to enjoy coming to my class. 4. Professional – I want my students to take me and my profession seriously.	Two of the words were the same and two were different. "Approachable" and "fun" remained the same while I added "intelligent" and "professional" in my new one. I left out "knowledgeable" and "caring." "Knowledgeable" and "intelligent" are very similar though.
ECSU-19	1. Energetic – always excited and bubbly (outgoing). 2. Caring – I care about the health and well-being of my students.	1. Energetic – I hope the students see how much energy and passion I have when I teach. 2. Knowledgeable – I want my	I had two of the same words, "energetic" and "caring." The second essay I used words "fun" and "knowledgeable" rather than "informative" and

	3. Informative – I give useful information and lifelong skills/activities. 4. Polite – I am well-mannered and courteous to all students and colleagues.	students to know how much I know about the subject. I want them to know that I know what I am doing. 3. Fun – I want my students to always have fun in my class. 4. Caring – I want and hope the students realize how much I care about them outside of the classroom as well as how much they can learn inside the classroom.	"polite." "Informative is similar to "knowledgeable" however, I think I learned that it's alright if some students think that I am a hard, mean teacher, I don't want the students to think they can walk all over me.. Yet I do still want the students to realize I have manners and treat students fairly.
ECSU-20	1. Fun – I want students to feel they have fun every time they are in my class. I want them to see me as a person that they can have fun with and enjoy being around. 2. Energetic – I want my energy to be contagious to all students and for them to see how passionate I am about what I do. I want them to follow my example and try hard and have	1. Caring – I care about the safety and feelings of my students. I want to make them feel comfortable in class. 2. Fun – I want the students to enjoy class and be able to have a good time. I want them to see me as a person they can enjoy having class with. 3. Understanding – I want my kids to see that I can relate to them. I want them to be able to know that	Some of the words changed, I used "enthusiastic" instead of "energetic" and "relatable" instead of "understanding," but the other tow, "fun" and "caring" were the same. The four concepts of what I hoped students would see in me has all stayed all the same. Even though some words differed all of my ideas remained unchanged on how I wanted to be perceived by my students.

136

	fun. 3. Caring – I want students to see me as a caring person who is concerned for the thoughts, feelings. And well-being of all students. I also want them to feel that they can easily come to me with help in any problems and concerns in any aspect of their lives. 4. Relatable – I want students to see that they can relate to me and that I know their situations and want to relate to them. I want them to feel that I understand them and know what they're going through.	they can come to me for help with any problems they have. 4. Enthusiastic – I want students to see that I love what I do. This will rub off on them and get them excited to learn.	

137

Sociometric Status

Sociometric Status - refers to the degree which children are liked or disliked by their peers.

- A child's likeability level by peer group ranges from *popular* (well liked by peers) to rejected (least liked by peers).

- Children who possess strong athletic competence usually rank highly in sociometric status.

- Children displaying poor athletic skills are often ranked low in sociometric status.

- Poorly skilled children are often ridiculed in physical activity situations.

- Humiliated children may withdraw or isolate themselves from physical activity (learned helplessness), which could further separate them socially from their peers.

Major factors affecting sociometric status:

1. Athletic competence

2. Physical appearance

3. Social skills

In order to work toward *success for all* in physical education, it is important for physical educators to identify and decrease the factors that may contribute to student loneliness and rejection in their classes. Students who experience rejection and loneliness are at greater risk for academic failure, juvenile delinquency, dropout, and mental health issues.

Dunn, J. C., Dunn, G. H., & Bayduza, A. (2007). Perceived athletic competence, sociometric status, and loneliness in elementary school children. *Journal of Sport Behavior*, 30, 249-269.

Learned Helplessness

The concept of learned helplessness (Seligman, 1975) may have application in understanding the experience of low-skilled students in PE. Learned helplessness is a perception of futility regardless of what one does, which could lead to a perceived lack of interest in performances and tasks and unwillingness to learn new skills (Martinek & Griffith, 1994; Walling & Martinek, 1995).

The pattern of learned helplessness could look like this:

Failure

↓

Belief in low ability

↓

Expectation of failure

↓

Reduction of effort/ Giving up

↓

Avoidance of public demonstration of low ability

(Adapted from Robinson, 1990).

"As an athlete relishes the anticipation of an upcoming competition, and a champion savors a win, the player who is physically awkward is concerned about upcoming forced participation in a game or sport and the anticipated expectation of failure" (Fitzpatrick & Watkinson, 2003, p. 292).

References

Fitzpatrick, D. A., & Watkinson, E. J., 2003). The livid experience of physical awkwardness: Adults' retrospective views. *Adapted Physical Activity Quarterly*, 20, 279-297.

Martinek, T. J., & Griffith III, J. B. (1994). Learned helplessness in physical education: A developmental study of causal attributions and task persistence. *Journal of Teaching in Physical Education*, 13, 108-122.

Robinson, D. W. (1990). An attributional analysis of student demoralization in physical education settings. *Quest*, 42, 27-39.

Seligman, M. E. P. (1975). *Helplessness: On depression, development, and death*. San Francisco: W. H. Freeman.

Walling, M. D., & Martinek, T. J. (1995). Learned helplessness: A case study of a middle school student. *Journal of Teaching in Physical Education*, 14, 454-466.

Carl Rogers: Student-Centered Education

Rogers believed in the student's innate capacity for growth and the importance of the *relationship* between the teacher and student. He contended that learning can occur more readily when the teacher can warmly accept students, provide unconditional positive regard, and empathize with students' feelings (Zimring, 1994). "When the teacher has the ability to understand the student's reactions from the inside, has a sensitive awareness of the way the process of education and learning seems *to the student*, then again, the likelihood of significant learning is increased" (Rogers, 1983, p. 125).

Rogers advocated three central concepts for humanistic education:

1. The teacher is congruent or integrated with the student. *The teacher is genuine.*

2. The teacher demonstrates unconditional positive regard for the student. *The teacher cares about the student's learning.*

3. The teacher experiences an empathic understanding of the student's point of view. *The teacher can put him/herself in the student's shoes.* (Rogers, 1983, Zimring, 1994).

References

Rogers, C. R. (1983). *Freedom to learn for the 80's.* Columbus, OH: Charles

    E. Merrill.

Zimring, F. (1994). Carl Rogers (1902-1987). *Prospects: the quarterly review*

    of comparative education (Paris, UNESCO: International Bureau of

    Education), 24, 411-422.

APPENDIX I

Follow-up interview with Dr. BC, Assistant Professor and instructor of control

groups one and two at University 3.

May 5 2009

TM: First of all I want to ask you about the statement in your [PESP 154] syllabus that reads: "This course is designed to help physical education teachers to acquire the knowledge, skills, and attitudes necessary to effectively teach physical education at the elementary level."

BC: Correct.

TM: Could you tell me about the attitudes part?

BC: Well I think there's the idea of just having the right disposition to be a teacher, that has been in the literature of late and you just want to make sure that students have those characteristics that are going to be conducive to learning for students and supportive of student learning.

TM: Do you have specific readings or something from the text? We all use the same text.

BC: Yes, certainly they read those chapters and I do supplement some readings, some of the motivational climate stuff by Todorovich – that one jumps out at my head right away. We talk about different teaching styles and just effective pedagogy and how to think through that. We talk a lot about Hellison's model of teaching personal social responsibility. I'm a big believer

144

in that and integrate that into my after school program certainly and bring that up in the classroom as well.

TM: I know you talk about content knowledge in one of your courses. Beyond content knowledge, what kinds of things do you think are important to teaching in your class?

BC: Well in 154 particularly is kind of designed for the pre-k through second grade experience, you know that basic foundation of understanding of the content is important and the fundamental motor skills. But just creating a learning environment that students want to explore and be physically active, and engage in physical activity and have fun with physical activity I think becomes important to that lifelong mover, so setting that framework for that. I'm a believer of trying to integrate subjects into physical education as well so we talk about how to bring in math and other topics as we do activities.

TM: Do you include any social constructs at all?

BC: No, not off the top of my head. I kind of took the beginning teaching standards this year and used those as my content area so we did a lecture on that and I put it into action in the gym throughout the semester so scientific and theoretical. We showed how to bring in biomechanics and exercise physiology in the gym; we did fitness and movement concepts and skill themes.

TM: How about psychological constructs?

BC: I don't spend much time on that, no.

145

TM: do you show any films?

BC: No.

TM: Do you include anything about gender at all?

BC: Some of the basic stats that we bring up at the beginning of the semester about teachers will call on boys more than girls, will allow boys to be more active and kind of disruptive in that sense. On the flip side they will allow girls to be more talkative in class. So we talk about some of those things that pull out in the literature and how that can impact us as teachers.

TM: do you discuss anything with diversity?

BC: No, not really with diversity.

TM: Ok thank you for your time.

BIBLIOGRAPHY

Aicinena, S. (1991). The teacher and student attitudes toward physical
education. *Physical Educator*, 48, 28-32.

Alterman, A. I., McDermott, P. A. Cacciola, J. S. & Rutherford, M. J. (2003).
Latent structure of the Davis Interpersonal Reactivity Index in
methadone maintenance patients. *Journal of Psychopathology and
Behavioral Assessment*, 25, 257-265.

American Alliance for Health, Physical Education, Recreation, and Dance.
(1999). *Physical education for lifelong fitness: The physical best
teacher's guide*. Reston, VA: Human Kinetics.

American Council on Exercise. (2008). Forget new math, this is new P.E.
Retrieved on 11/19/2008 from
http://www.acefitness.org/healthandfitnesstips.

Ames, C. (1984). Achievement attributions and self-instructions under
competitive and individualistic goal structures. *Journal of Educational
Psychology*, 76, 478-487.

American Obesity Association. (2002). Fact sheet: Obesity in youth. Retrieved
April 14 from
http://www.obesity.org/subs/fastfacts/obesity_youth.shtml

Anderson, D. R. (2002). The humanity of movement or "It's not just a gym class." *Quest*, 54, 87-96.

Anderssen, N. (1993). Perceptions of physical education classes among young adolescents: Do physical education classes provide equal opportunities to all students? *Health Education Research: Theory & Practice*, 8, 167-179.

Aspy, D. N., & Roebuck, F. N. (1977). *Kids don't learn from people they don't like*. Amherst, Massachusetts: Human Resource Development Press.

Aspy, D., & Roebuck, F. (1983). Our research and our findings. In C. Rogers (Ed.), *Freedom to learn for the 80's* (pp. 199-217). Columbus, OH: Charles E. Merrill.

Barnett, M. A., & Bryan, J. H. (1974). Effects of competition with outcome feedback on children's helping behavior. *Developmental Psychology*, 10, 838-842.

Barnett, M. A., Matthews, K. A., Corbin, C.B. (1979). The effect of competition and cooperative sets on children's generosity. *Personality and Social Psychology Bulletin*, 5, 91-94.

Barnett, M. A., Matthews, K. A., & Howard, J. A. (1979). Relationship between competitiveness and empathy in 6 – and 7-year-olds. *Developmental Psychology*, 15, 221-222.

Barnett, M. A. (1987). Empathy and related responses in children. In N. Eisenberg & J. Strayer (Eds.), *Empathy and its development* (pp. 146-162). Cambridge: Cambridge University Press.

Batson, C. D., Polycarpou, M. P., Harmon-Jones, E., Imhoff, H. J., Mitchener, E. C., Bednar,L. L., Klein, T. R., & Highburger, L. (1997). Empathy and attitudes: Can feeling for a member of a stigmatized group improve feelings toward the group? *Journal of Personality and Social Psychology*. 72, 105-118.

Bekiari, A., Heropoulou, H., & Sakellariou, K. (2005). Perceived aggressive physical education teacher communication, student state satisfaction and reasons for discipline. *Italian Journal of Sport Sciences*, 12, 73-78.

Bellini, L. M., Baime, M., & Shea, J. A. (2002). Variation of mood and empathy during internship. *Journal of the American Medical Association*, 287, 3143-3146.

Berman, S. (1998). The bridges to civility: Empathy, ethics, and service. *The School Administrator*, 55, 27-32.

Blitzer, L. (1995). "It's a gym class... What's there to think about?" *Journal of Physical Education, Recreation and Dance*, 66, 44-48.

Brown, J., D'Emidio-Caston, M., & Benard, B. (2001). *Resilience education*. Thousand Oakes, CA: Corwin Press.

149

Bush, C. A., Mullis, R. L., & Mullis, A. K. (1999). Differences in empathy
between offender and nonoffender youth. *Journal of Youth and
Adolescence*, 29, 467-478.

California Department of Education (CDE). (2001). *California physical fitness
test: Report to the governor and legislature.* Sacramento, CA:
California Department of Education Standards and Assessment
Division.

California Department of Education (CDE). (2005). *California physical fitness
test: A study of the relationship between physical fitness and academic
achievement in California using 2004 test results.* Sacramento, CA:
California Department of Education Standards and Assessment
Division.

Carlson, T. B. (1995). We hate gym: Student alienation from physical
education. *Journal of Teaching in Physical Education*, 14, 467-477.

Castelli, D. M., Hillman, C. H., Buck, S. M., & Erwin, H. E. (2007). Physical
fitness and academic achievement in third- and fifth-grade students.
Journal of Sport & Exercise Psychology, 29, 239-252.

Centers for Disease Control and Prevention. (1997). Guidelines for school and
community programs to promote lifelong physical activity among
young people. Retrieved August 9, 2007 from

http://www.cdc.gov/mmwr/preview/mmwrhtml/00046823.htm

Ciccomascolo. L. & Riebe, D. (2006). Setting the stage for physical activity
   for secondary students. *Journal of Physical Education, Recreation and
   Dance*, 77, 34-39.

Coe, J. (1984). Children's perception of physical education in the middle
   school. *Physical Education Review*, 7, 120-125.

Corbin, C. B. (2002). Physical education as an agent of change. *Quest*, 54,
   182-195.

Cothran, D. J. (2001). Curricular change in physical education: Success stories
   from the front line. *Sport, Education, and Society*, 6, 67-79.

Covington, M. V. (1985). Strategic thinking and the fear of failure. In J.W.
   Segal, S. F. Chippman & R. Glasser (Eds.), *Thinking and learning
   skills: Vol. 1* (pp.389-416). Hillsdale, N.J.: Lawrence Erlbaum
   Associates.

Cutcliffe, J. R., & Cassedy, P. (1999). The development of empathy in students
   on a short, skills- based counseling course: A pilot study. *Nurse
   Education Today*, 19. 250-257.

Cutforth, N., & Parker, M. (1996). Promoting affective development in
   physical education: The value of journal writing. *Journal of Physical
   Education, Recreation and Dance*, 67, 19-23.

Cruz, B. E., & Patterson, J. M. (2005). Cross-cultural simulations in teacher
    education: Developing empathy and understanding. *Multicultural
    Perspectives, 7*, 40-47.

Darling-Hammond, L., & Sykes, G. (2003). Wanted: A national teacher
    support policy for education: The right way to meet the "Highly
    Qualified Teacher" challenge? *Education Policy Analysis Archives,*
    11. Retrieved January 29, 2007 from http://epaa.asu/epaa/v11n33/

Davis, M. (1980). A multidimensional approach to individual differences in
    empathy. *JSAS Catalogue of Selected Documents in Psychology, 10,*
    85.

Davis, M. H. (1983). Measuring individual differences in empathy: Evidence
    for a multidimensional approach. *Journal of Personality and Social
    Psychology.* 44, 113-126.

Davis, M. H., & Franzoi, S. L. (1991). Stability and change in adolescent self-
    consciousness and empathy. *Journal of research in Personality, 25,*
    70-87.

Davis, M. H. (1996). *Empathy: A social psychological approach.* Boulder, CO:
    Westview.

DeCorby, K., Halas, J., Dixon, S., Wintrup, L., & Janzen, H. (2005).
    Classroom teachers and the challenges of delivering quality physical

education. *Journal of Educational Research*, 98, 208-220.

Dewar, A. M., & Lawson, H.A. (1984). The subjective warrant and recruitment into physical education. *Quest*, 36, 15-25.

Dewey, J. (1966). *Democracy and Education: An introduction to the philosophy of education.* New York: Free Press. Originally published 1916/1944.

Dewar, A.M., & Lawson, H. A. (1984). The subjective warrant and recruitment into physical education. *Quest*, 36, 15-25.

Dobkin, D., & Cooper, B. (Producers), Gillespie, C (Director). (2007). *Mr.Woodcock* [Motion picture]. United States: New Line Cinema.

Donaldson, M. (1978). The shape of minds to come. *Children's minds.* New York, NY: W.W. Norton.

Doud, G. (Writer). (1991). *Classroom of the heart* [Motion picture]. (Available from Focus on the Family, Colorado Springs, CO 80995).

Duncan, C. A., Nolan, J., & Wood, R. (2002). See you in the movies? We hope not! *Journal of Physical Education, Recreation and Dance*, 73, 38-44.

Dunn, J.C., Dunn, G.H., & Bayduza, A. (2007). Perceived athletic competence, sociometric status, and loneliness in elementary school children. *Journal of Sport Behavior*, 30, 249-269.

Eisenberg, N., & Strayer, J. (Eds.). (1987). *Empathy and its development.*
Cambridge: Cambridge University Press.

Emde, R. (1989). Mobilizing fundamental modes of development: Empathic
availability in therapeutic action. *Journal of American Psychoanalytic
Association*, 38, 881-913.

Espelage, D. L., Mebane, S. E., & Adams, R. S. (2003). Empathy, caring, and
bullying: Toward an understanding of complex associations. In
D. Espelage & S. Swearer (Eds.). *Bullying in American
schools: A social-ecological perspective on prevention and
intervention* (pp. 37–61). Mahwah, NJ: Erlbaum.

Evans, J., & Roberts, G. C. (1987). Physical competence and the development
of children's peer relations. *Quest*, 39, 23-25.

Ferguson, K. J., Yesalis, C. E., Pomrehn, P. R., & Kirkpatrick, M. B. (1989).
Attitudes, knowledge, and beliefs as predictors of exercise intent and
behavior in schoolchildren. *Journal of School Health*, 59, 112-115.

Feshbach, N. D., & Feshbach, S. (1969). The relationship between empathy
and aggression in two age groups. *Developmental Psychology*, 1(2),
102-107.

Feshbach, N. D., & Feshbach, S. (1987). Affective processes and academic achievement. *Child Development*, 58, 1335-1347.

Fitzpatrick, D. A., & Watkinson, E. J. (2003). The livid experience of physical
awkwardness: Adults' retrospective views. *Adapted Physical Activity
Quarterly*, 20, 279-297.

Fox, K. (1988). The child's perspective in physical education part 5: The self-
esteem complex. *British Journal of Physical Education*, 19, 247-
252.

Fox, K., & Biddle, S. (1988). The child's perspective in physical education
part 3: A question of attitudes? *British Journal of Physical Education*,
19, 107-111.

Freire, P. (1983). *Pedagogy of the oppressed*. New York: Continuum.

Gard, M. (2006). Why understanding itself is physical education's greatest
challenge: A response to Himberg. *Teachers College Record*. Retrieved
March 5, 2008 from http://www.tcrecord.org.

Garner, R. (1990). When children and adults do not use learning strategies:
Toward a theory of settings. *Review of Educational Research*, 60,
517-529.

Gerdes, D. A. (2001). Leadership education: Physical activity and the affective
domain. *The Physical Educator*, 58, 78-85.

Gibbons, S. L., & Bressan, E. S. (1991). The affective domain in physical education: A conceptual clarification and curricular commitment. *Quest*, 43, 78-97.

Gifford-Smith, M. E., & Brownell, C. A. (2003). Childhood peer relationships: Social acceptance, friendships, and peer networks. *Journal of School Psychology*, 41, 235-284.

Goodman, D. J. (2000). Motivating people from privileged groups to support social justice. *Teachers College Record*, 102, 1061-1085.

Grineski, S. (1992). What is a truly developmentally appropriate physical education program for children? *Journal of Physical Education, Recreation and Dance*, 63, 33-35, 60.

Grineski, S., & Bynum, R. (1996). Same old stuff: All I really needed to learn, I didn't learn in PE. *Journal of Physical Education, Recreation and Dance*, 67, 60-61.

Håkansson, J., & Montgomery, H. (2003). Empathy as an interpersonal phenomenon. *Journal of Social and Personal Relationships*, 20, 267-284.

Hatcher, S. L., Nadeau, M. S., Walsh. L. K., Renyolds, M., Galea, J.,& Marz, K. (1994). The teaching of empathy for high school and college students: Testing Rogerian methods with the interpersonal reactivity index. *Adolescence, 29*, 961-974.

Himberg, C. (2005). The great challenge for physical education. *Teachers College Record*. Retrieved March 5, 2008 from \http://www.tcrecord.org.

Hinkle, D. E., Wiersma, W., & Jurs, S. G. (1998). Applied statistics for the behavioral sciences, fourth edition. Boston: Houghton Mifflin.

Hoffman, M. L. (1987). The contribution of empathy to justice and moral judgment. In N. Eisenberg & J. Strayer (Eds.), *Empathy and its development* (pp. 47-80). Cambridge, UK: Cambridge University Press.

Hoffman, M. L. (2003). *Empathy and moral development: Implications for caring and justice*. Cambridge, UK: Cambridge University Press.

Huitt, W. (2005). Important affective dispositions: Optimism, enthusiasm, and empathy. *Educational Psychology Interactive*. Retrieved January 3, 2007 from http://chiron.valdosta.edu/whuitt/col/affsys/optenth.html

Hunt, L. (2007). *Inventing human rights*. New York: W.W. Norton & Company.

Iannotti, R. J. (1985). Naturalistic and structure assessments of prosocial behavior in preschool children: The influence of empathy and perspective taking. *Developmental Psychology*, 21, 46-55.

Janzen, H. (2003/2004). Daily physical education for K-12. Is government

legislation in sight? *Physical Education and Health Journal*, 69, 4-
12.

Jensen, E. (2005). *Teaching with the brain in mind*. Alexandria, VA:
Association for Supervision & Curriculum Development.

Kalliopuska, M., & Roukonen, I. (1993). A study with a follow-up of the
effects of music education on holistic development of empathy.
Perceptual Motor Skills, 76, 131-137.

Kegan, R. (1982). *The evolving self: Problem and process in human
development*. Cambridge, MA: Harvard University Press.

King, A. C. (1991). Community intervention for promotion of physical activity
and fitness. *Exercise and Sports Science Reviews*, 19, 211-259.

Kohlberg, L. (1981). *The philosophy of moral development: Moral stages and
the idea of justice*. San Francisco: Harper & Row.

Kohlberg, L., & Mayer, R. (1972). Development as the aim of education.
Harvard Educational Review, 42, 449-496.

Kohn, A. (1986). *No contest: The case against competition*. Boston: Houghton
Mifflin.

Kohn, A. (1990). *The brighter side of human nature: Altruism and empathy in
everyday life*. New York: Basic Books.

Kohn, A. (1998). *What to look for in a classroom ... And other essays*. San Francisco: Jossey-Bass.

Koka, A, & Hein, V. (2006). Perceptions of teachers' positive feedback and threat to sense of self in physical education: A longitudinal study. *European Physical Education Review*, 12, 165-179.

Kremer, J. F., & Dietzen, L. L. (1991). Two approaches to teaching accurate empathy to undergraduates: Teacher-intensive and self-directed. *Journal of College Student Development*, 32, 69-75.

Laker, A. (1996). Learning to teach through the physical as well as of the physical. *British Journal of Physical Education*, 27, 18-22.

Laker, A. (2000). *Beyond the boundaries of physical education: Educating young people for citizenship and social responsibility*. London: Routledge.

Lee, A. M., Carter, J. A., & Xiang, P. (1995). Children's conceptions of ability in physical education. *Journal of Teaching in Physical Education*, 14, 384-393.

Litvack-Miller, W., McDougall, D., & Romney, D. M. (1997). The structure of empathy during middle childhood and its relationship to prosocial behavior. *Genetic Psychology Monographs*, 123, 303-324.

Locke. L. F. (1992). Changing secondary school physical education. *Quest*, 44, 361-372.

Martinek, T. J., & Griffith III, J. B. (1994). Learned helplessness in physical education: A developmental study of causal attributions and task persistence. *Journal of Teaching in Physical Education*, 13, 108-122.

McAllister, G., Irvine, J. J. (2002). The role of empathy in teaching culturally diverse students. *Journal of Teacher Education*, 53, 433-443.

McBride, R. (1995). Critical thinking in physical education... An idea whose time has come! *Journal of Physical Education, Recreation and Dance*, 66, 21-23.

McCallum, J. (2000). Gym class struggle. *Sports Illustrated*, 92(17), 82-96.

Mergendoller, J. R., & Packer, M. J. (1985). Seventh graders' conceptions of teachers: An interpretive analysis. *The Elementary School Journal*, 85, 581-600.

Michigan Association for Health, Physical Education, Recreation, and Dance (Producer). (1997). *No more dodgeball: The new phys. ed in Michigan schools* [Motion picture]. (Available from Media Technologies, 143 Bostwick N.E.Grand Rapids, MI 49503)

Miller, P. A., & Eisenberg, N. (1988). The relation of empathy to aggressive and externalizing/antisocial behavior. *Psychological Bulletin*, 103, 324-344.

Morrell, M. E. (2003, August). *Education, empathy and democracy.* Paper presented at the annual meeting of the American Political Science Association, Philadelphia, PA.

Mowrer-Reynolds, E. (2008). Pre-service educator's perceptions of exemplary teachers. *College Student Journal*, 42, 214-224

National Association for Sport and Physical Education (2001). *Physical education is critical to a complete education.* [Position paper]. Reston, VA: Author.

National Association for Sport and Physical Education (2001 -2008). *Position Statements and Guidance Documents.* Retrieved March 30, 2008 from http://www.aahperd.org/NASPE/template.cfm?template=position-papers.html

National Association for Sport and Physical Education (2004). *Moving into the future: National standards for physical education* (2nd ed.), Reston, VA: Author.

Noblit, G. W., Rogers, D. L., & McCadden, B. M. (1995). In the meantime: The possibilities of caring. *Phi Delta Kappan*, 76, 680-685.

Nodings, N. (1992). *The Challenge to Care in Schools: An Alternative Approach to Education.* New York: Teachers College Press.

Noddings, N. (1998). Teaching themes of care. In K. Ryan & J. M. Cooper (Eds.), *Kaleidoscope: Readings in education,* 8th Ed., (pp. 471-477). Boston, Houghton Mifflin.

O'Hara, M. (1989). Person-centered approach as conscientização: The works of Carl Rogers and Paulo Freire. *Journal of Humanistic Psychology,* 29, 11-36.

O'Keefe, P., & Johnston, M. (1989). Perspective taking and teacher effectiveness: A connecting thread through three developmental literatures. *Journal of Teacher Education,* 40, 20-26.

Oswald, P. (2003). Does the interpersonal reactivity index perspective-taking scale predict who will volunteer time to counsel adults in college? *Perceptual and Motor Skills,* 97, 1184-1186.

Page, R. M., & Scanlan, A. (1994). Childhood loneliness and isolation: Implications and strategies for childhood educators. *Child Study Journal,* 24, 107-119.

Patterson, C. H., & Purkey, W. W. (1993). The preparation of humanistic teachers for the next century. *Journal of Humanistic Education and Development,* 31, 147-155.

Pinderhughes, E. B. (1979). Teaching empathy in cross-cultural social work. *Social Work*, 24, 312-316.

Pluvoise, D. (2006, July 12). Sen. Barack Obama urges students to reverse 'empathy deficit.' *Diverse: Issues in higher education*. Retrieved June 11, 2009 from http://diverseeducation.com

Portman, P. A. (1995). Who is having fun in physical education classes? Experiences of sixth-grade students in elementary and middle schools. *Journal of Teaching in Physical Education*, 14, 445-453.

Portman, P. A. (2003). Are physical education classes encouraging students to be physically active?: Experiences of ninth graders in their last semester of required physical education. *Physical Educator*, 60, 150-161.

Pulos, S., Elison, J., & Lennon, R. (2004). The hierarchical structure of the interpersonal reactivity index. *Social Behavior and Personality*, 32, 355-359.

Robinson, D. W. (1990). An attributional analysis of student demoralization in physical education settings. *Quest*, 42, 27-39.

Rogers, C. R. (1983). *Freedom to learn for the 80's*. Columbus, OH: Charles E. Merrill.

Rovengo, I., & Bandhauer, D. (1997). Norms of the school culture that facilitated teacher adoption and learning of a constructivist approach to physical education. *Journal of Teaching in Physical Education*, 16, 401-425.

Sagi, A. & Hoffman, M. L. (1976). Empathic distress in the newborn. *Developmental Psychology*, 12, 175-176.

Sanders, S. W. (1996). Children's physical education experiences: Their interpretations can help teachers. *Journal of Physical Education, Recreation and Dance*, 67, 51-56.

Satcher, D. (2005). Healthy and ready to learn. *Educational Leadership*, 63, 26-29.

Seligman, M. E. P. (1975). *Helplessness: On depression, development, and death*. San Francisco: W. H. Freeman.

Shapiro, J. E. & Lawson, H. A. (1982). Locus of control: A neglected measure for affective development in physical education. *Physical Educator*, 39, 126-130.

Siedentop, D., & Locke, L. (1997). Making a difference for physical education: What professors and practitioners must build together. *Journal of Physical Education, Recreation and Dance*, 64, 25-33.

Simner, M. L. (1971). Newborn's responses to the cry of another infant. *Developmental psychology*, 5, 136-150.

Siu, A. M. H., & Shek, D. T. L. (2005). Validation of the Interpersonal
Reactivity Index in a Chinese context. *Research on Social Work
Practice*, 15, 118-126.

Smith, S. J. (1991). Where is the child in physical education research? *Quest*,
43, 37-54.

Smith, T. K., & Cestaro, N. G. (1998). *Student-centered physical education:
Strategies for developing middle school fitness and skills*. Champaign,
IL: Human Kinetics.

Solomon, G. B. (1997). Fair play in the gymnasium: Improving social skills
among elementary school students. *Journal of Physical Education,
Recreation and Dance*, 68, 22-25.

Solomon, G. B. (2004). A lifespan of moral development in physical activity.
In M. Weiss (Ed.), *Developmental sport and exercise psychology: A
lifespan perspective* (pp. 453-474). Morgantown, WV: Fitness
Information Technology, Inc.

Sosa, D. (1995). *How the brain learns*. Va.: National Association of Secondary
School Principals.

Stelzer, J. (2005). Promoting healthy lifestyles: Prescriptions for physical
educators. *Journal of Physical Education, Recreation and Dance*,
76, 26-29, 44.

Stevens-Smith, D. A. (2002). Why your school needs a quality physical education program. *Principal*, May, 2002, 30-31.

Stork, S., & Sanders, S. (1996). Developmentally appropriate physical education: A rating scale. *Journal of Physical Education, Recreation and Dance*, 67(6), 52-58.

Stout, C. J. (1999). The art of empathy: Teaching students to care. *Art Education*, 52(2), 21-34.

Symons, C. W., Cinelli, T. C., & Groff, P. (1997). Bridging health risks and academic achievement through comprehensive school health programs. *Journal of School Health*, 67, 220-227.

Tinning, R., & Fitzclarence, L. (1992). Postmodern youth culture and the crisis in Australian secondary school physical education. *Quest*, 44, 287-303.

Tishman, S., & Perkins, D. N. (1995). Critical thinking and physical education. *Journal of Physical Education, Recreation and Dance*, 66, 24-30.

Twenge, J. (2006). *Generation me: Why today's young Americans are more confident, assertive, entitled – and more miserable than ever*. New York: Simon and Shuster.

United States Department of Health and Human Services. (1996). *Physical*

activity and health: A report of the Surgeon General. Atlanta, GA: U.S.
Department of Health and Human Services, Centers for Disease
Control and Prevention, National Center for Chronic Disease
Prevention and Health Promotion.

United States Department of Health and Human Services. (2000). *Healthy
people 2010* (2nd ed.).Washington DC: U.S. Government Printing
Office.

Villaire, T. (2001). The decline of physical activity: Why are so many kids out
of shape? *Our Children, 26*, 8-10.

Virshup, A. (1999). Why Janey can't run. *Women's Sports and Fitness, 2*,
130-139, 152.

Walling, M. D., & Martinek, T. J. (1995). Learned helplessness: A case study
of a middle school student. *Journal of Teaching in Physical Education,
14*, 454-466.

Waxler, C. Z., Yarrow, M. R., Brady-Smith, J. (1977). Perspective-taking and
prosocial behavior. *Developmental Psychology, 13*, 87-88.

Weiss, M. R., & Duncan, S. C. (1992). The relationship between physical
competence and peer acceptance in the context of children's sport
participation. *Journal of Sport & Exercise Psychology, 14*, 177-191.

Weiss, M. R., & Stuntz, C. P. (2004). A little friendly competition: Peer

relationships and psychosocial development in youth sport and physical
activity contexts. In M. Weiss (Ed.) *Developmental sport and
exercise psychology: A lifespan perspective* (pp. 165-196).
Morgantown, WV: Fitness Technology, Inc.

Westcott, W. L. (1992). High school physical education: A fitness
professional's perspective. *Quest*, 44, 342-351.

Whitehead, M. (2000). Aims as an issue in physical education. In S. Capel
& S. Piotrowski (Eds.), *Issues in physical education* (pp. 7-21).
London: Routledge/ Falmer.

Williams, N. F. (1992). The physical education hall of shame. *Journal of
Physical Education, Recreation and Dance*, 63, 57-60.

Williams, N. F. (1994). The physical education hall of shame, part II. *Journal
of Physical Education, Recreation and Dance*, 65, 17-20.

Williams, N. F. (1996). The physical education hall of shame, part III:
Inappropriate teaching practices. *Journal of Physical Education,
Recreation and Dance*, 67, 45-48.

Wispé, L. (1987). History of the concept of empathy. In N. Eisenberg &
J. Strayer (Eds.), *Empathy and its development* (pp. 17-37).
Cambridge: Cambridge University Press.

Wood, G. (2004). A view from the field: NCLD's effects on classrooms and

schools. In D. Meier and G. Wood (Eds.) *Many Children Left* Behind.
Boston: Beacon Press 33-50.

World Health Organization. (2007). *"Stop the global epidemic of chronic
disease" New report, preventing chronic diseases: A vital investment
estimates hundreds of billions of dollars at stake.* [Data file]. Available
from World Health Organization Web site,
http://www.who.int/mediacentre/news/releases/2005/pr47/en/print/html

Yarrow, M. R., Scott, P., & Waxler, C. Z. (1973). Learning concern for others.
Developmental Psychology, 8, 240-260.

Yarrow, M. R. & Waxler, C. Z., with Barrett, D., Darby, J., King, R., Pickett,
M., & Smith, J. (1976). Dimensions and correlates of prosocial
behavior in young children. *Child Development.* 47, 118-125.

Zimring, F. (1994). Carl Rogers (1902-1987). *Prospects: the quarterly review
of comparative education (Paris, UNESCO: International Bureau of
Education),* 24 (3/4), 411-422.